True Hard

"This personal account of a tour of duty in Vietnam is told with great courage and authenticity—it is harrowing, humanizing and eye-opening. I'm honored to know Larry Lelito and call him a dear friend. His tireless work to support veterans and their families and his dedication to his community has earned him a reputation as a great man here in Northern Michigan. Larry has laid his heart and his story on the line with his book, TRUE HARD. We all stand to benefit from his experience. It should be required reading in high schools across our country, and for our political leaders as well. This book is a compelling, poetic read and it is accessible to folks from all walks. Our society as a whole should be fully aware of the human cost of war, and of the need for support and healing for our communities of combat veterans. TRUE HARD is a testimony that will help our country and our leadership down that healing path."
—Seth Bernard, artist, educator, and Founder, Earthwork Music

"Take a clear and profound look into the mind of a combat veteran. TRUE HARD is a masterful collection of stories told in an authentic voice, and the presentation of these stories in free verse poetry emphasizes the gravity of the topics discussed. Mr. Lelito is a beacon of hope for veterans in search of healing."
—Michael J Berkowitz, student at Berklee College of Music

Private Larry Lelito, December 1965.

True Hard

For the Rest of Our Lives

A Marine's story of War, Survival, and Healing
From his Tour in Vietnam

Larry Lelito

Poems written in Larry's words by
Terry Wooten

Parkhurst Brothers Publishers
MARION, MICHIGAN

© Principal text copyright 2017 by Larry Lelito. All rights reserved under the laws and treaties of the United States of America and all international copyright conventions and treaties. No part of this book may be reproduced in any form, except for brief passages quoted within news, blogs, reviews, or similar works, without the express prior written consent of the author.

www.parkhurstbrothers.com

Printed in the United States of America

First Edition, November 2018

Printing history: 2018 2019 2020   8 7 6 5 4 3 2 1

Cataloging in Publication Data:
Lelito, Larry, 1946-
p. cm.
True Hard: A Marine's story of War, Survival, and Healing From his Tour in Vietnam
1. Memoir–Vietnam War 2. Poetry–Vietnam War 3. Oral Tradition–Vietnam War 4. Nonfiction–PTSD   I.–Title.

ISBN: Trade Paperback978162491-UUU-U

Parkhurst Brothers Publishers believes that the free and open exchange of ideas is essential for the maintenance of our freedoms. We support the First Amendment of the United States Constitution and encourage all citizens to study all sides of public policy questions, making up their own minds.

Transcription and text arranged by:	Terry Wooten, poet/bard
Cover design by:	Linda D. Parkhurst
Page design by:	Susan Harring
Production management by Parkhurst Brothers Publishers:	Ted Parkhurst
Photographs courtesy of:	Larry Lelito

112018

This book is dedicated to my wife,

Theresa

She is the love of my life
and has had my six since
the summer of 1969.

A Note on Permission

Of the poems in this collection, those below have been featured by the *Traverse City Record Eagle* in Terry Wooten's "Lifelines" column.

Christmas Present
A Soldier's Elegy for Martin Luther King, Jr.
The Hole
Snails
Water
The Buddha Statue

Contents

Changed   10
Introduction   11
Prologue, Part 1   The General and His Wife   16
Prologue, Part 2   For the Rest of Our Lives   17
Marine Corps Construction Battalion   21
Infantry   22
Survive, Evade, Resist, Escape   24
The Ghost   26
Captured   27
Escape   29
Tortured   30
Buried Alive   33
Tear Gas   34
Vietnam   35
A Mess   37
The People   38
Like Death   39
Squad Leader's Advice   42
Primitive   43
To Survive   44
The Third Day   45
Doctor   47
1966   50
Agent Orange   51
Water   53
Mother Mary   57
Leech Attack   59
We Carried Salt   61
Mosquitoes, Snakes and Spiders   62
Five Percent   63
Sharp   65
Beer   66

The Hole   67
Shit Bird   70
Operation Hastings Begins   72
Listening Post   75
Blood Trails   77
The Skull   79
The Rockpile Encounter   80
Thieves   82
A Mass Grave   83
Wounded   85
Sick   89
Malaria   91
The Hospital   93
Bad Shape   94
Intensive Care Unit   95
Emergency Landing Zone   96
Ambush   98
The Pilot   101
Pfc. Martinez   103
L/cpl. Starcher   103
First Confirmed Kill   105
Numb   109
The Buddha Statue   110
The Vietcong Knew   114
The Outpost   115
Christmas Present   118
Dog Food and Protests   121
Sniper Training   122
The Course   123
Scout Sniper   126
Sniper   127
Revenge   128
The Shot   131
Fight and Hurt   133

The Little Boy   133
Snails   138
A Box Mine   141
Alone   143
Hate   144
I Just Can't   145
Sergeant E-5   146
Nightmares   147
Home   149
San Francisco   152
Bedlam   154
A Soldier's Elegy for Martin Luther King, Jr.   155
Busted   159
R and R   161
Epilogue   163
Theresa: Party House   163
Theresa: In Love   165
Theresa: Early Marriage   167
Theresa: The List   168
Post-Traumatic Stress Disorder   169
What Was This   171
Terrible Stories   172
I'll Never Go Back   173
Now   174
The Ceremony   174
Healing   177
Foundation for Healing   179
The Man in the Arena, By Theodore Roosevelt   183

Changed

I was nineteen
when my Hispanic buddy was killed,
and seven or eight other buddies were killed
or wounded in an ambush.

When I say wounded I'm not talking scratched.
I mean blown up bad.
1966 changed my life.
I never had the same passion for living again.

When you start fighting for your own preservation
 there's a big difference.
You turn into a different kind of person.

You don't make friends
or rely on other people.
I became a one-man deal.

I left my unit and became a sniper.
I grew cold, hard and ruthless.

That's just how fate was.
I figured the more enemy I killed
the chances of me coming home were better,
and the chances of them killing
another American soldier was less.

Introduction

The overly familiar cliche, "War is Hell" is also true of the aftermath of war. Only the aftermath of war lasts forever.

The purpose of this book is to pass on the knowledge of how to deal with the trauma of war. This is a first-hand history of what war was like and how I dealt with the effects of the physical and emotional issues.

During the 1950s and 1960s our country was under constant threat of war against the Communist-ruled countries. Several times a week we would practice air raid drills at school in preparation for a nuclear attack by the Soviet Union.

From 1945 to 1990 we were in a Cold War which was political hostility between the Soviet Bloc countries and the U.S.-led Western powers. During 1950 to 1953 we fought a war against the Communists of North Korea who were supported by China and the Soviet Union. Two and a half million people lost their lives. On October 4, 1957 the Soviets launched a satellite called Sputnik. The first artificial satellite to orbit earth caused the arms race to intensify and heightened the Cold War.

In April of 1961 the C.I.A. was involved in The Bay of Pigs invasion of Cuba in an attempt to throw out the Communist regime. The mission failed.

October 1962 was one of the most terrifying times in American history. The Soviet Union was transporting nuclear weapons by ships in an attempt to install them in Cuba. A U.S. blockade stopped them.

On November 22, 1963, John F. Kennedy, our 35th President, was assassinated by Lee Harvey Oswald, a suspected Soviet agent.

March 8, 1965, the First Marines landed in Vietnam and the first large-scale battles against the North Vietnamese Army began.

The politics and true reasoning of the war in Vietnam were not things that I questioned. I felt that it was my duty to help defend our country. I joined the Marines and went on active duty November 22, 1965. The Vietnam War was in its early stage. I believed our leaders when they told us that we had to take a stand against the Communists in Southeast Asia, and that it would only take a few months to run the North Vietnamese Army out of South Vietnam, and our job would be over.

My country, the United States of America, trained me how to fight and kill. I was sent to Vietnam in May of 1966. I was 19 years old. The war lasted nine more years.

I've been part of war all my life. My father and four of his brothers fought in close combat during World War II. I grew up around these guys and learned at an early age what the trauma and stress of war can do to a person.

My father, Stanley, served in General Patton's 3rd Army as a combat engineer. The engineers were well respected because they often worked in front of the infantry, clearing mine fields, building roads and bridges, blasting obstacles, and often engaging the enemy. He was awarded a Silver Star by General Patton for heroism during the Battle of the Bulge.

In the spring of 1945, Patton's Army was marching through collapsing Germany. The engineers were in front sweeping for minefields near the town of Weimar. They came upon the German Nazi Buchenwald concentration camp. My father was one of the first Americans to enter the compound. He was haunted for the rest of his life by what he saw and experienced that day.

My Uncle Florek served with an Army artillery regiment. He was captured by the Japanese in the Battle of Corregidor Island in Manila Bay, Philippines on May 6, 1942. He spent the remainder of the war as a slave laborer. When he returned to America, he lived a rough life. Unable to fit into society, he lived like a hobo.

My Uncle Peter served in the Navy as a seaman on a battleship that was torpedoed and sunk by a Japanese submarine in the Pacific Ocean. Seriously injured, he spent several months recovering on a hospital ship. After he was put on a ship that was returning to America, that ship was torpedoed and sunk. He made it to an overcrowded lifeboat where he joined some men who had to hang over the side. Sharks appeared and started biting them. Peter received a serious shark bite on his thigh just before they were rescued. When he finally made it home, he spent most of his life in and out of hospitals, suffering from Traumatic Brain Injury and combat PTSD.

My Uncle Hank was the captain of a naval destroyer that searched out and fought German U-boats on the North Atlantic Ocean. A U-boat was a deadly German submarine that was feared by all who sailed the North Atlantic. The endless stress of war, cold winter, rough seas, and lack of supplies took a toll on the captain and crew. When the war was over, Hank raised his family in Boston. Sometimes he would ride his Harley to our house in Detroit. He would give me a ride and I asked him, "Isn't it a long way to ride a motorcycle from your house to ours?"

He said, "Yes, but the ride frees my mind." Sometimes my father would be on the phone and would tell my mother, "Hank's in the V.A. Hospital again."

I'd ask, "Why is Hank in the hospital?"

They would say, "He has shell shock; you're too young to understand." But I did.

My Uncle Chris was an Army M.P. who guarded German prisoners being transported from Europe to America. The prisoners were confined below deck in a holding area. Sometimes they would fight or get out of line, and Chris would have to enter the holding area to handle the situation. It wasn't safe to get close with a firearm, so he would enter the cage with a hammer and knock out the ones that were causing trouble.

My father and uncles have all passed away. As I write this, I think about the amazing stories that were lost with them. I truly wish they had left a diary, a book or notes, something for their family, future generations, and the community, to look back on for first-hand experience of their time in World War II.

I hope this book might serve as an encouragement for other veterans to write their stories, even if they're grizzly and graphic. Writing about war is difficult but therapeutic. People want to know about it. How else are our veterans going to be understood?

Around 1974 the State of Michigan sent a questionnaire to Vietnam veterans regarding combat stress symptoms. My wife, Theresa, and I didn't understand what Post-Traumatic Stress Disorder was, but I filled out the form and tested positive on every question for PTSD.

I hadn't associated with any other veterans since being discharged from the Marines. I didn't have anybody to confer with, so I handled it as best I could alone until a notice in our local newspaper stated there was going to be a meeting of veterans who were exposed to Agent Orange. I had been in a highly exposed area, so my wife and I decided to attend. I was very uncomfortable being around other vets but stuck it out and learned a lot. Some of the other vets were from the Traverse City area and we started associating a little bit. We began to realize that we were all dealing with the issues that were listed on the PTSD test.

We soon formed a Chapter of the Vietnam Veterans of America. The more members that joined, the more we realized that we needed some professional help. One of our out-of-town members was a Vietnam combat veteran who was also a clinical psychologist and had studied war trauma. We hired him to come to Traverse City once a month to counsel us on PTSD. He was helping us. After a year or so he asked five of us if we would like to go through peer counselor training. We agreed and went through what I would call an extensive PTSD course.

After we completed the training we filed for a 501c3 tax status for our Welcome Home organization for helping troubled veterans. We staffed an office in Traverse City with a secretary and one of the five members as a full-time employee. This was the start of one of the first vet centers in Michigan. It was 1989. Since this time, I have engrossed myself in learning about PTSD, and have counseled and mentored many veterans. My combat experience gives me a great deal of credibility for helping veterans.

I have a large network of people from all walks of life that know me as a veteran who is knowledgeable on veterans' issues. I have been called upon as a first responder to help with many serious issues. Doctors, politicians, lawyers, therapists, law enforcement, et cetera contact me at any time of the day or night to help with someone who wants to harm themselves or others. It might be someone that is in need of emergency financial assistance, or someone that just needs a person to talk to. I keep my veteran business strictly confidential unless it is in regard to harming one's self or others. Then proper authorities will be notified and involved.

The narratives that follow were written in free verse poetry. I chose this way of telling my story in straightforward English. These are complicated tales with deep meaning that needed to be told in an easy-to-read style.

My friend Terry Wooten, an acclaimed poet-bard, interviewed and recorded me over the past seven years. He transcribed my words and arranged them into his unique style of poetry.

Larry Lelito
Traverse City, Michigan,
August, 2018

Prologue, Part I

The General and His Wife

At the college in 1991
they had a five-part program on Vietnam
with various speakers.

A South Vietnamese general with his wife
were presenters one night,
talking about their culture.

In 1966 there was a horrific battle
in the Quang Tri province
where this general was in charge
of the South Vietnamese Army.

We got air-lifted in
on a large number of the enemy.
From the beginning
it was absolutely terrible,
a constant battle.

I asked this general
if he remembered that battle,
I forget the name of the village.

He answered, "Oh yes, I do remember that.
Our troops were guarding the left flank
of that operation."

I asked, "Do you remember
 anything about it?"
"No, not really," he replied.
"My wife and I were down in Saigon
at a ballroom dance."

My blood started boiling,
and he could tell.
I was remembering that battle
and what had happened.
This S.O.B. was in Saigon
at a ballroom dance,
instead of being with his troops.

I quit going to the college programs.
I couldn't deal with it anymore.

Prologue, Part II

For the Rest of Our Lives

The 4th Marines were pushing
the enemy to us.
We were on a blocking force
with the 1st Marines
in a position headed towards this village.

You could see the enemy
trying to escape.
They were being squeezed
and panicked.
Finally they stood their ground.
We had to do battle with them.

As we got closer to the village
we started taking casualties.

A medivac chopper came hovering
into the landing zone
to pick up the wounded.
It got hit in the air
and caught fire.

A big flame was shooting out.
We thought
the helicopter had a flame thrower
if there was such a thing.
But it became engulfed in fire
three or four hundred feet
in the air.

The crew started bailing out
to their deaths.
After the medivac crashed
the 2nd platoon tried to rescue any survivors.

The 2nd platoon got hit
and were pinned down by the chopper
in a cultivated field.
They took a lot of casualties.

I was in the 1st platoon
that needed volunteers
to go in and help.
I got volunteered by my commander.

I went in with a black corpsman
and a few other guys.
There were dead and wounded
in the field
around the burning chopper.

While the corpsman tried to help
I laid down a base of fire for him.

We were under assault
by five or six Chicom machine guns,
small arms fire
and a grenade fight.
We got reinforcements,
called in gun ships
that sprayed the area,
and got the wounded out before dark.
We left our dead
till the next morning.

The enemy was causing a ruckus
in the village.
A lot of them were in there
and pushed the civilians out.

We called in Phantoms,
Marine fighter-jets
to drop napalm on them.
A lot of us were so close to the area
where it was falling,
we had to bury ourselves
in the sand
to keep from being burned alive.

Next morning,
because I'd been there the night before,
I was the point man
who led everybody who felt rested
back into this battlefield.

The medivac chopper had cooled off
and was melted to a shell.
Inside were the skulls
of the pilot and copilot.

We needed to retrieve their skulls
for identification.
I crawled in
this molten-metal burned-out frame,
grabbed the skulls,
and brought them out.
We put them into a bag
with their dog tags.

The crew chief who bailed out
hit the ground so hard
his torso was planted in the ground
with his legs up over his head.
His face was charred,
and his 38 pistol was still in his hand.

We got him
and the rest of our dead
out of there,
and went on to hunt
for what was left of the enemy.

During the night they'd left.
Thirty or forty of them were dead
in this trench.
We recovered the machine guns
they'd used on us.
Our engineers came in
and blew up their bunkers.
The battle was over,
except in our minds
for the rest of our lives.

Marine Corps Construction Battalion

I was 18.
I wanted to join the Navy
and go into the Seabees.
I had a construction background
and figured I'd do good.

The Navy
recruiter was locked up for lunch.
Across the hall
was a Marine Corps recruiter.
He said, "Come over and talk to us
while you're waiting."

They asked me about my background
and schooling.
I'd graduated from high school
and worked construction all my life
in our family business
in the Detroit area.

The recruiter said, "You'd do good
in the Marine Corps Construction Battalion,
but you'd have to sign up for three years
instead of two.
We run a lot of heavy equipment,
clear jungles,
and build airports.
You're probably going to wind up in Vietnam."
I accepted that.
They talked me into joining the Marines.

I wasn't going to be an infantryman.
I would be a heavy equipment operator.
The recruiter guaranteed that.

So I signed up
in late summer 1965.
I turned 19 on October 17,
and left for Boot Camp in November.
I turned 20 in Vietnam.

Infantry

It was on a Sunday in Boot Camp.
We'd go out on the street,
outside of the Quonset huts
where we slept,
sit on five-gallon buckets,
clean our rifles and write letters.

They were passing out MOS's
which was going to be your military occupation.
Mine said, "Private Lelito-0311."
That was infantry.

"No, there's a mistake,"
I said, "I signed up
to be a heavy equipment operator."
"Too bad, you're 0311 now."

I insisted to see the head man
in charge.
They had office hours
for you to make an appointment
to see the captain.
I walked into his office a few days later.

The officers were angry at me,
but I didn't want to be an infantryman.

I gave the captain a spiel
about signing up for an extra year
because the recruiter guaranteed
I would go into construction battalion.

The captain looked at me and said, "Are you through?"
"Well yes," I said, "Are you
going to sign me up for construction battalion?"

He said, "Private you're insulting me.
You're a piss poor human being.
You know that?
You've been selected by
the United States Marine Corps
to go into the proudest outfit
the Marine Corps has,
and that's the infantry.
Now get your ass out of my office
and go to work.
You're in the infantry."

Survive, Evade, Resist, Escape

I trained for the infantry
instead of construction battalion,
but there's different stages of training.
You could go regular,
advanced,
or into a more intense infantry training
which was a SERE course:
Survive, Evade, Resist, Escape.

I had no choice
and didn't know what SERE was.
I didn't know anything.

After advanced training
50 of us out of the whole battalion
were put on a helicopter
and taken to a remote island
somewhere outside of Camp Pendleton.
To this day I don't
know where it was.

The object was to live off the land
and make your way to a certain point
without getting captured by the enemy
they called Aggressors.

Escape was impossible.
They knew exactly where you were going to go,
and you were on an island.
They gave us each one carrot
and two cups of rice
in a sack you carried on your belt.

For five days
you were supposed to survive
on trapped animals.
We caught a couple rattlesnakes
and cooked and ate them.
We finally caught a rabbit,
and wound up down in this jungle area
for a class.

There was this real hardcore instructor
 who told us everything to do with a rabbit.
First thing he did
was squeeze the rabbit's head
till it's eyes popped out.
He pulled the rabbit's eyes out
and ate them
in front of us.

"You eat every part of this," he lectured,
"You need the nutrition and protein,
bla, bla, bla."
I thought, "That ain't
ever going to happen."

The Ghost

We called him The Ghost.
This British Commando,
a lead combat soldier,
would sneak around at night,
and you couldn't see him.

He was training us in jungle warfare.
On a night mission
he taught us how to do things in the dark.
We returned to the same area
the next day.

He said, "Now gentlemen,
do you have any questions?"
"No sir."
"Well, you're all prisoners of war."
What the hell
did that mean?

Captured

Out of the jungle from all sides
came guerrilla fighters
dressed like the Vietcong,
and started beating the living shit out of us.

If you didn't do exactly what they wanted,
they rapped you on the head
with their rifles.
You'd better mind these guys
or you were going to get hurt.
We had bloody noses
and bumps and bruises
on our heads and bodies.
We were captured.

They marched us down this trail
in a special way.
You had to hold your hands underneath
 the chin of the guy in front of you
in a real tight formation.
You didn't dare move out of it
or they'd hurt you.

We reached this prison camp,
a mock set-up
of a North Vietnamese camp.
We were put in a barbed wire compound
with loud speakers
preaching propaganda,
telling us we were prisoners of war,
and urging black guys
to join up with them
because of white privilege
doing them wrong.

After questioning,
they gave us a big pot of water
with a sack of rice.
We were all hungry and built a fire
to heat the water,
and poured the rice in the pot.

Our meal was cooking away,
almost done,
when a guard kicked it over
to demoralize us.

Escape

The idea of this training was
if you could escape
you didn't have to go through the last
couple days.
You'd be shipped back to Camp Pendleton
and could go on liberty.

I was quite athletic in high school,
agile and strong,
and on the gymnastic team.
Sitting on the edge of my group,
checking out the set-up,
I figured I could run down the hill,
jump up,
put my foot on the barbed wire,
and propel myself over
the roll of concertina wire,
sharp as razors.

I'd sneak out through the jungle
and get away.
There weren't any guards out there.

I made a break for it,
caught my toe on a peg of barbed wire,
and it flipped me down.
The guards caught me right away.

I was someone
to make an example of.

Tortured

They took me away from the prison compound
down to this grass shack
like they'd have in Vietnam.

The guards stood around
questioning and telling me
if I signed this paper
to be a Communist Liberation Army soldier,
I would be fed,
taken care of;
I could join their ranks.
I said, "No, I can't do that."

Three or four guys grabbed me
and took me down to this shallow creek
maybe a foot deep
and all rocky.

They took a stick
a little bigger than a broom handle,
put it between the back of my legs
and bent me over backwards
until I was in terrible pain
from my knees.

Six guys were working on me.
They stripped me,
stretched me out
and spread my legs apart.

One guy between my legs
made a fist with his middle knuckle protruding
like an arrow,
and began beating my groin
right above my pubic hair.
It was excruciating pain.

Two guys were holding my arms,
a guy was holding my head,
a guy was sitting on my chest.
The other guy carried a five gallon can
down to the creek,
filled it with water
and began waterboarding me.

With the guy beating on my groin,
I was in terrible pain.
I was drowning.
They were holding me down.
I couldn't fight it.

They would ease up and say,
"Are you ready to sign?"
I broke, "I'll sign. I'll sign. I'll sign."

I could hardly walk.
They dragged me up to the shack.
This leader
whatever his rank was,
sat me down
and said, "That was terrible
what happened to you.
We don't want that to happen again."

"No Sir, certainly not," I answered.
"Would you like something to eat?"
I said, "Yes."
He gave me some water
and a C ration,
and I started eating.

He talked about the People's Liberation Army,
how they were this noble group.
"Here's the paper and pen.
If you sign this, you'll be all set.
You won't have to go back in the prison.
We'll put you through some training,
and you've already been trained
by the Marines.
You'll have rank and control of men."

I only had two days left
in that camp.
If I signed that paper
it wouldn't look good for me.
I was in a Catch-22 position.

"Listen Sir," I said, "I'm weak
and my mind's not working properly.
If I could have a couple days
to figure this out."

He jumped up
and smacked me in the face.
I fell down on the floor.
Two guys came running in.
They grabbed me
and dragged me back down the hill.

Buried Alive

They took me to a 20' by 20' area
that looked cultivated.
They handed me a shovel
and told me to dig a rectanglar-shaped hole.

In boot camp
you were given all kinds of odd jobs
if you did something wrong.
I figured it was a digging punishment.
So I dug this hole.

A couple guys dragged out a box,
put me in it,
and buried me alive.

It was cramped, stuffy and dark
except for two small holes
where I could see daylight.
I was in the box maybe an hour,
but it seemed like 24 hours.

They'd see me trying to breathe
fresh air through one hole,
and they'd kick sand down
into my nose.
They poured water down the hole.
I was buried
with water up to my neck,
trying to survive.

They'd say, "Have you had enough?"
I thought they were going to kill me,
and said, "Yes."

They dug me out
and took me down to the creek again.
I thought, "Oh, my God."

But this time
a Marine Corps Major was there watching.
He saw them bend me over backwards
and stretch me out,

but they weren't torturing me
like before,
and I could take it.

Afterwards they led me back
to the prison camp.
I could hardly walk
and almost crawled part way.
I watched them torture other guys.
I wasn't the only one.

Tear Gas

We had to go inside a gas chamber
with gas masks on.
There were no windows
and 20 men fit in there.
We stood in two lines of ten
facing each other.

They threw this gas in on a burner
or something.
I don't know how they ignited it.

It was so dark
you couldn't see anything.
The instructor said,
"All right, take your gas masks off
and sing The Marine Corp's Hymn!"

You choked through it
and put your gas mask back on
while exhaling
like they'd taught you.

If you did it right
you were only in there ten seconds
but some guys couldn't manage
and were in there longer.

Some guys puked.
It was enough to know
you never wanted to be gassed.
That was the end of our SERE course.

Vietnam

After training I headed for Vietnam.
We landed in Hawaii, then Guam,
and stopped in Okinawa
for a few days training.

From Okinawa we flew to Vietnam
on a commercial airliner.

We stepped off the plane,
breathed that air
and gasped.
The heat parched our throats and noses.
It was unbelievable.
None of us had ever experienced
heat like that.

It was miserable all the time,
except during the monsoon
when the temperature got down
to maybe 48 degrees at night,
which was enough to chill you
after that hot muggy weather.

There were 360 to 370 of us
in a line
getting our orders.
They split us all up
to different places.
It was chaos.

I was standing there waiting
to find out
where I was supposed to go.

This guy who'd been there several months
was standing behind watching
what was going on,
and struck up a conversation with me.
He was a wounded Marine.
A punji stake had gone through his foot,
and he was healing up.
He was trying to fill me in
on things,
and I was listening.

The guy on the loud speaker
on the stage in front of us
asked, "Does anybody know how to type?"
I mentioned to the wounded Marine
I'd taken a semester of typing
in high school.

He said, "Raise your hand!
Tell him yes! Tell him yes!"
I said, "I don't want to sit in some tent
and type over here."

It was the worst mistake
I ever made.

A Mess

We were saving them from communism,
but they didn't want to be saved.
The whole thing was a lie.
We were in cahoots with criminals
running South Vietnam
who asked us for help.

The Communists had a treaty
after the French War.
The country was cut in half
by the Demilitarized Zone in 1954.
South Vietnam wanted their share,
but the Vietcong started infiltrating
and causing havoc.

We sent 80 Army captains over
as advisors to help train their army,
and supplied them with equipment:
artillery, mortars and rifles.

A lot of Catholic churches were built,
I assume because of Kennedy.
The enemy would tear them down.
Some of the advisors started getting killed,
and the conflict escalated.

Our leaders, Westmoreland and Johnson,
thought that America was invincible,
thought we'd go in there and kick ass.
It didn't work out like that.
The Vietnamese people were too tough.
The war started out to end Communism,
and ended up a mess.

The People

The people were used to war
and fighting.
The French War
had only ended ten years earlier.

The Vietnamese were not like us.
When they found a home
the whole family lived there
generation after generation,
whether it was a little spot of ground
or in a village with a hut.

Members of their families
had fought against the French,
and people in their families
had been killed by the French.

Now it wasn't the French War.
It was the American War,
and most sided with the North Vietnamese.
They secretly supplied them
with food and ammunition,
and patched up their roads.

The enemy didn't have spotter planes
or need sophisticated equipment.
They had people
on the ground
to spy on us.

You never knew who to trust.
Little girls or old women
might open up on you.
They were part of the resistance.

Like Death

I got orders to go to Second Battalion,
First Marines,
Hotel Company,
about 100 miles away.
Five of us got on a chopper.

It was a tent camp set up
with no protection.
Only ten guys were in the whole camp.
The rest were out fighting
a battle nearby.
You could hear gunshots in the distance.

We were told to go
to this supply tent
and get our gear.
Inside the tent was in disarray.
In the States
a supply area was all organized and labeled.
Here stuff was just piled up.

The guy gave me an old, beat-up M-14 rifle
with a cartridge belt.
He threw a flak jacket at me.
It was caked
with coagulated blood inside
and fairly fresh.
It was blown to hell
and had a piece of a man's intestine
or something from inside a person
still stuck to it.

I said, "What the hell is this?"
"That's your flak jacket," he answered.
I said, "I'm not taking this damn thing."
"That's all you got.
Take it and clean it up," he said.

I walked back to my tent
and looked around.
There were bandoleers,
machine gun bullets hanging

here and there,
and grenades everywhere
tossed at random.
There was no order to anything.

We were ordered out to the Landing Zone.
My squad I'd been attached to
was coming back
out of the field.

The chopper came in.
The earth was red clay in this area,
and the chopper was blowing
red dust around.
Off the chopper came these guys
walking towards where I was standing.

I'll never forget seeing those men
for the first time.
They looked like death,
like they were already dead guys.
Their eyes were different
from anything I'd ever seen.
Their clothes were pure white
from dried sweat,
and their pants were all ripped up.
Their rifles were shiny like chrome.
Over there, rifles rusted quick.

You had to use steel wool,
so everybody's M-14
had the bluing sanded off.
These guys would barely talk to me.
All these impressions were hitting me
like *this is not normal.*

Squad Leader's Advice

I lucked out.
My squad leader was from
my hometown in the Detroit area.
He'd been in the Marine Corps for ten years
and was a corporal.

He'd fought at the Bay of Pigs
in southern Cuba in 1961,
and a couple other skirmishes
around the world
before Vietnam.

He was a seasoned hard-core dude,
and he showed me the ropes.

He told me, "We're here for one reason,
to survive.
And to survive you're going to have to kill.
Get that in your head right now!
If it comes down to the point
that it's either you or him,
don't even think twice.
Do it!"

I kept those words in my head.
He rotated back home
a month after I got there.

Primitive

I was in a line company,
an infantry unit;
2nd Battalion, 1st Marines
Hotel Company, 1st Plt.

Whenever they'd spot a large group
of the enemy,
they would call in our company
and drop us right on top of them.

We'd have to battle it out.
It was crazy
and out of control.

In a firefight
you just hoped to make it out alive.

There were bullets and shooting all over.
Wounded men were screaming.
Shrapnel was flying through the air.

Nobody knew
where anybody was at.
An all-out-battle
is as primitive as you're ever going to get.

You didn't know
if you were going to get shot
by your own men,
or if you were going to shoot them.

To Survive

We tried to survive,
and did what we were told
best we could.

You looked out
for the other man.
A lot of times
you were more concerned
about the other guys
than you were about yourself.
Everybody was the same.

You turned into a real strong brotherhood
looking out for one another.
It's a bond like you have with your own family.

We lived out in the bush
sharing stuff.
We ate with the same spoon,
and might share a can of peaches.

If one guy ran out of ammunition
you'd share your ammunition with him.
You counted on a buddy
to supply you with toilet paper.

You depended on each other
like you've never depended
on anybody before.

Anything
to do with combat is extreme.

The Third Day

I'd been with Hotel Company three days
and got to know a few guys.
Some of them would talk to me,
but others wouldn't.
I was a "FNG,"
a f---ing new guy,
green and inexperienced,
and caused a certain amount of danger
being with them.

We got called out
on my first mission.
An observation plane had spotted
a group of North Vietnamese Army soldiers,
supposedly 30 of them.
We climbed on choppers
and flew out to the area
where they'd been seen.

It was a battalion operation,
and Hotel Company was the blocking force.
The numbers didn't turn out right.
There were more than 300 of them.

When the battle started
with bullets coming in,
I was unaware.
It sounded like bees going by.

Guys were hollering at me,
"Get down! Get down!
You're going to get killed!"

Our blocking force didn't see much action,
but Echo Company
and Gulf Company got massacred.

I don't know exactly what happened
to Echo Company.
They took heavy casualties.
But Gulf Company got caught
right in the middle of a rice paddy.

They were walking across a dike
when the enemy opened up on them.
Within minutes
Gulf Company was down
with heavy casualties.

The battle dispersed.
I found out quick
the enemy always had an exit.
They'd hit and run.

It was over with.
Everything was quiet
except for choppers coming in for
the wounded.

We got orders to swing around
and come down the same path,
the same rice paddy dike
where Gulf Company got hit.

Around the dike
an area half the size of a football field
was covered with blood and body parts.
There were tourniquets,
battle wraps,
and all types of gear lying around
blown up or shot up.

When the whole mess was over
there were 18 killed
and 46 severely wounded.
That was my third day
with Hotel Company.

Doctor

I'd only been there a couple weeks
and was totally ignorant
about the Vietnamese people.

I'd already seen combat,
but as far as the countryside
and what the people were going through,
I was dumb.

Fifteen of us were on patrol.
It was a cooler day
and we were in a nice spot,
a rolling farm field
of foot-high grass.

Our position was to wait on this berm,
and watch for the enemy
being pushed to us.
On top this berm was a trail
villagers used.

Nothing was happening,
and we'd sat there for a few hours.
It was getting towards evening.

I looked down the trail
and saw somebody hobbling towards us,
closer and closer.
It was a kid
with the front of his right foot blown off
by a land mine
the enemy had put out.

The kid passed a couple other guys
who ignored him,
and walked right up to me.

He had a crutch made out of a stick,
and his damaged foot was muddy.
I waved for him to come closer
so I could look at his wound.

The rest of the guys told me
to leave him alone
and ignore him.
I wasn't tough enough,
or war wary yet
to do that.
I didn't disobey orders.
Nobody ordered me.

I took my canteen and washed his foot.
The damage was bad.
The bones were protruding,
and the foot had been healing
under a black dirty scab.

I washed the wound best I could,
bandaged his foot with a battle wrap,
gave the kid a couple aspirin,
and sent him on his way.

The kid hobbled off,
and our patrol kept waiting
in our position.

I heard a commotion
coming down the trail.
What the hell!
A whole village of sick people were coming
towards us:
pregnant women,
people with other wounds,
or malaria.

They were saying, "Doctor, doctor,"
in Vietnamese.
They thought I was a doctor.
I could've been
with all my first aid training.
I was well-advanced over anything they had.

"We told you so," the other guys said.
"You can't treat them.
There's nothing we can do."
We had to pick up and leave.

We couldn't deal with them.

I thought, "What in God's name
kind of war is this?"

The country was so poor and behind.
Our large deployment of troops
began in late 1965.
Before that it was just advisors
and trainers.
This was early 1966,
so the war had been going on
for only five or six months.
Most of the villages we entered
had never seen Americans before.

1966

In July 1966
we weren't set up that well.
The enemy had better weapons
than we did.

We wore the same pair of pants
for a couple months,
and the same boots.
You were never dry during the monsoons.

You lived off what you could carry
in your pack.
You'd carry as much ammunition
and as many grenades as you could.
If you were ordered to carry flares,
you'd have flares,
and set aside some rations.

We were issued M-14's,
a good rifle that never jammed.
It was accurate
and fully-automatic.
You could fire 20 rounds fast,
750 rounds a minute cyclic rate.
A lot of times
you weren't shooting at a target,
just spraying the jungle.

Then they gave us M-16's
which was a shitty weapon.
They were always jamming.
Nobody trusted them.

Agent Orange

We'd go through a village area
in the middle of summer
with gardens all over.
We'd eat the cucumbers and melons
and other vegetables.

It was the growing season,
but the vines were all wilted
like it was fall.
We couldn't figure it out.

We didn't know
our planes were dropping defoliants.

Later on we moved into the jungle
and a liquid would drip on us
from the trees.
We started getting blisters.
It affected black guys a lot worse.

Our leaders told us
it was French blister gas
the enemy was using.

We found out later
it was Agent Orange
our planes had sprayed on the jungle
to kill it,
and they sent us in there.

We used the empty barrels
to warm water for showers,
and we cut empty Agent Orange barrels
in half to cook in.

Water

We were on a long-range patrol,
a 30-mile hike,
loaded down to the gills.
There were 40 of us.
It was hotter than hell.
It seemed like 130 degrees.
I'd only been over there three weeks.

Our mission was to climb
to the top of this mountain.
We didn't have to rope ourselves together.
There were vines
growing out of the rocks.

When it's that hot
and you're loaded down,
every man needs a gallon of water
a day.
We each carried four canteens.

By the time we reached our position,
Our water was almost depleted.
Our orders were to stay up there
till we were resupplied,
but we lost radio contact.
There was no way
to give our coordinates,
so we couldn't get resupplied.

We were stuck there through the night.
By the second day
we were really tight for water.

Three o'clock in the afternoon
guys were becoming delirious.
The lieutenant in charge
had his orders to stay,
but we had to get out of there
or we were going to cook.

We climbed down
looking for water.

I wasn't acclimatized to the heat
and was dying of thirst.
I knew I didn't have much longer.
I could hardly walk anymore.

I told the squad leader
if I conked out to just leave me.
I knew they wouldn't,
but I didn't want to be a burden
on the rest of the guys.

"Hang on, hang on," he said.
"Let me see if I can find a little water."

He walked up the line
and came back with a guy I'd never seen before.
This guy was different.
He didn't look like the rest of us.
He had brown eyes
and wasn't carrying a rifle,
his clothes were cleaner than ours.

He handed me this canteen
and said, "Marine, this canteen is half full,
but you can't drink any of it.
Some of the other guys are going to need it.
Take a swig,
slosh it around in your mouth
and spit it back in.
We need every drop,
but this will help you."

I put that canteen to my mouth.
The warm water was slimy.
Other guys had probably done the same thing.
I was so tempted
to drink the whole contents.
I was so dehydrated
my mouth was like leather
and my lips were parched.

I spit the water back in the canteen,
and he walked off.
I never saw that guy again.

It was very strange.
I call him an angel.
What else?

We came to a bomb crater
that had been there for a while.
A thousand-pound bomb
makes a hole the size of a house.
It was full of filthy water with green scum on it.

There was a water buffalo standing in the crater
with animal waste floating around.

I got down on my knees,
pushed the scum away with my hands
to clear the water
which was orange
from the color of the soil.
You could see little bugs shooting around.

We'd filled our canteens
and dropped in the purifying pills.
The sergeant was yelling,
"Don't drink that water!
You've got to wait 20 minutes
for the halazone to kick in!"
But I didn't have 20 minutes.

I stuck my head in the water,
chugged it down.
It was like drinking sweet warm tea
and it kept me alive.

A month later
I came down with malaria.
I'm surprised I didn't get liver fluke.
Worms were a big thing over there.
You didn't know when you got 'em.
You could carry them for thirty years
and then die.

Every time I go to the faucet
and turn it on,
I think of that time.
I don't take a cold glass of water
for granted at all.

Mother Mary

The enemy had ravaged this village
and destroyed a Catholic church.
Hotel Company got orders
to sweep through the area
and follow them.

We were traveling light,
but packed to the gills with ammunition,
expecting a fight.
As usual is was real hot.
Villagers had cisterns out,
so we were able to fill our canteens
with their water.

It was uncomfortable in the dry heat,
moving fast
trying to catch up with the enemy
who'd been there the day before.

We traveled a couple miles by foot
into the village
to check out this new church.
It wasn't masonry,
but more of a pole building,
and was in shambles,
full of bullet holes.

Some guys went inside.
I stood guard
making sure nobody sneaked up on us.

One Marine named Martinez
came out very upset.
"They shot Mother Mary," he said.
Things were happening fast.
It didn't dawn on me
he meant Jesus's Mother.

Other guys were coming out
so I walked in
thinking I'd find a dead human being.
There was a statue of the Virgin Mary
with a bullet hole
between her eyes.
The whole place was riddled.
Most of the Hispanic guys were Catholic
and it bothered them bad.

We left that building
and moved on
until we came upon this weird construction
that was a Buddhist temple.
We searched through there
into this back room.
Several monks
were having an opium party
lying on cots all dazed out.

The lieutenant ordered us
to search the room quick
and get back out,
so we wouldn't get high off the smoke.

The monks were no threat to us
so we left them alone.

Leech Attack

We moved out
in the dead of the heat.
Four or five hours later we held up
until further orders.

There was this low spot
that was shaded
next to the road we were standing on.
To get out of the hot sun
we went into this low spot,
a jungle-type bamboo thicket.
It was cooler down in there.

We didn't have packs.
We took off our ammunition belts
and laid back.
After a few minutes
guys started to feel themselves and scratch. What the hell.
I looked around.

Worms an inch and a quarter long
were falling out of the trees
and crawling across the ground
like caterpillars towards us.

They were tree leeches
that are attracted by the heat of a body
to feed on,
which was us.
Leeches were crawling all over us
biting and trying to dig in.
They wouldn't let loose
if you poured salt on them.
We had to evacuate that shaded place.

That type of leech
tries to find every orifice in your body.
They'll crawl in your eyes,
your nose, your ears,
and go up your anus or penis.

We didn't wear underwear
and had faulty issue jungle clothes.
We'd sweat
and it would rot the armpits and crotches
out of our uniforms,
some worse than others.
Mine were pretty much ripped open.
The leeches had easy access
to our private parts.

Back up into the sun
guys were grabbing their asses and penises.
The leeches were trying to crawl in.
We were itching everywhere.
I pulled and burned
a lot of them off myself.

We had to check
each other's scrotum and asshole.
We had no tools
to probe a guy's rectum.
We took two 30 caliber bullets
and used them like chopsticks
with the pointy end
to spread a guy's butthole
and look up in there.

If a leech was up in there,
you took a lit cigarette,
burned it, and pulled it out.
That was a terrible experience.

I had tree leeches on me several times,
but that was extreme.

We Carried Salt

Another kind of big black leech
lived in rice paddies,
and would get on us,
as we walked through the water.
I had them on me several times.

They could get sixteen inches long,
and would wrap themselves twice
around your ankles above your boots.

They'd hook on
and start sucking your blood.
You were miserable all the time
going through brush
and rice paddies.

A leech bite wasn't noticeable
when you were in combat,
alert and ready all the time.

When you finally got somewhere to rest,
you'd reach down to scratch your leg,
and feel a big black leech.

They came off easy with salt.
We always carried salt.
Soon as you put salt on them,
they'd shrivel up and fall off.

Mosquitoes, Snakes and Spiders

It seemed like everything over there
was trying to screw you over,
whether it was the heat,
the constant swarms of mosquitoes,
or the tarantulas.
There were four kinds of poisonous snakes.

I saw cobras,
but the worst was a bamboo viper
called a "two-stepper."
Word was, if you got bit by one,
you'd go two steps
and you were dead.
I never knew anybody that got bit
by a bamboo viper,
but I saw them.

I saw spiders in the jungle
with bodies big as baseballs.

At night you'd walk through the jungle
following the river bottoms,
and their webs stretched across the water.

It was impossible
to travel through the jungle.
You couldn't even hack your way with a machete.
You'd make ten feet
in half a day.
It was that thick.

So the enemy
and you traveled on river bottoms
under a jungle canopy.
The walking was easy
with rocky bottoms
and good fresh water,
but the bugs and spider webs were awful.

Five Percent

Before you go into a tough situation
everybody wonders
what their strengths are going to be.

Ninety-five percent
can deal with it.
No matter how horrible battle is
you'll find an inner strength.

I was in bad situations a lot of times.
You kind of get used to it
after a while.

Five percent
of the guys
can't hack it.
They go into what's called "battle fatigue."

They can be in one battle
and ruined the rest of their life.
It screws their minds up bad.

We had this real nice guy with us,
18 or 19 years old.
His dream in life
was to be a Marine.

He got sent to our unit
same time I did.
We'd been in Vietnam about a month
when we got into a serious combat situation.

We had a North Vietnamese Battalion trapped.
We had them surrounded.
These guys had to fight their way out
and did everything they could.
The fighting was fierce.

There was a lot of death,
a lot of people blown up
and shot up.

This guy took one look
at all the enemy bodies,
and it flipped him out.
He couldn't help it.

A couple days later on the same operation
in the middle of the night,
he started hollering for his mother
and crying.

Here we were on a listening post
out in the jungle,
and this guy had flipped right out.
He wasn't faking.
You could tell it was the real thing.

We got him back to the rear.
They tried to give him some counseling
and send him back,
but he just wasn't cut out for battle.

Sharp

I know a lot of pot and drug use went on
over in Vietnam,
but not out in the bush
until later in the war.

In the jungle, in 1966-67,
you didn't have access to anything except beer.

Out in the field
you wanted your mind sharp.
Your life and your buddies' lives
depended on it.

You were on the job
in a combat zone,
and needed to be aware
of everything that went on
around you.

After being there awhile
it became like a sixth sense.
You felt when things weren't right.
Your hair might stand up
on the back of your head.
You'd get chills down your spine.

That was the time to be aware.
If you were under the influence
of any sort of substance,
it took your edge away
and decreased your chances 50 percent.

Beer

There's more to war than duking it out,
being in firefights or combat
all the time.

There were food and water issues.
You wore dirty clothes
and got eaten up by mosquitoes and bugs.
You lived out in the elements
and it exhausted you.

The military loves to drink.
It's a drinking outfit.

I don't care if
it's the Army, Navy, Marines,
Air Force, or Coast Guard,
drinking's a pastime.
They can turn you into a professional drinker.

The military's going to get you beer
wherever you're at.

You could be in the hottest combat situation,
and when the battle was over
they'd send hot beer
before ammunition.
I saw it happen.

The Hole

I'd already seen heavy combat.
We were on a sweep through a village
in the midst of a battle.

The Vietcong and Vietnamese people
all had holes they crawled into.
In this village there was a hole.
My sergeant said, "Lelito,
throw a grenade in there!"

I grabbed a grenade off my chest
and pulled the pin
to chuck it in the hole.
But I saw an old man in there waving, "No."
I held the spoon trigger down.

The sergeant yelled, "Throw the grenade!"
I didn't.
He yelled, "I'm giving you an order! Throw it in!"
I saw a woman behind the old man.
I disobeyed sergeant's orders again.

Out of this hole crawled twelve people,
all women and kids
behind this old man.
To this day I cringe
when I think of that moment.
I still get emotional
and almost cry.

Sergeant stood there looking mean,
but he knew I'd done the right thing.

That old man helped everybody out,
and they ran off
behind the lines
in the direction we motioned.

That old man looked into my eyes,
nodded his head
and motioned for me
to throw the grenade in the hole.
I nodded back,
and he took off.
I'll never forget the look on his face.

The canister on Lelito's belt here is a gas grenade, used to clear bunkers, tunnels, etc. It didn't do permanent damage, but made breathing unbearable. "I refused to use explosives when I was concerned about hurting innocents."

The two little girls holding babies cared for the younger ones while their parents worked their rice fields and gardens. The haircuts made it easier to remove lice.

Shit Bird

He didn't seem able to do anything right,
was always screwing up,
not motivated,
or on the ball.
Our squad leader didn't like him.
I hate to call anybody a Shit Bird,
but that's the slang we used.

Shit Bird was on a machine gun team
during the battle
at Quang Tri.

His platoon went in first
trying to rescue survivors.
During the battle
they got pinned down,
gunned down big time
and took a lot of casualties.

His team leader was shot in the leg
and couldn't do anything.
This guy picked up the machine gun
and advanced on the enemy
alone.

There were several machine guns and automatic rifles
shooting at him.
I couldn't believe it.
Shit Bird had bullets kicking up dust
all around him.
He was wide out in the open
carrying that M-60,
shooting from the hip,
and walking right towards them.

There would've been many more casualties
if it hadn't been for him.
I could tell you
about several of those kinds of guys.

Operation Hastings Begins

We'd just gotten off a major battle
in the Thua Thien province
that lasted a week or more.
We were beat up.

We returned to an Air Force base
in the far north of South Vietnam
called Dong Ha.
It was as far north as you could get
without being in North Vietnam.

We rested up inside the base
and held security
for the Air Force for a few days.
We got to take showers
and eat good food.
We were living large.

You never knew ahead
where you were going to be
from one time to the next.
Guys in the field don't get information
about what the generals are planning.
Mentally you weren't prepared.
They didn't want to frighten you.

On July 15 at 2 o'clock in the morning
we were told to saddle up,
which meant get your gear on
to go into combat.

On the tarmac
a supply truck came around
and loaded us with claymores mines,
grenades,
all the ammunition we could carry,
flares, and a few rations.
We filled two canteens
and sat waiting.

There were hundreds of us on that tarmac.
Chinook helicopters came in,
loaded us up
and headed out in the middle of the night.
We didn't know where we were going
or what we were getting into.

After 15 or 20 minutes
the enemy started shooting at us.
You could look out the windows
and see bluish-green tracers
coming and going up.

A bullet hit our prop
and the chopper started vibrating—
not like it was going to crash—
but there was a change
in the way it felt.

One Chinook did get shot down.
Thirteen men and four crew members were killed
in the crash.

We landed in a flat place,
in an area without a lot of foliage,
just short grass
with mountains around us.
It was totally dark and chaotic.
Guys were running all over.
We had no protection at all,
being wide out in the open.

The choppers took off
and the enemy started shelling us.

I was by myself
and could hear other guys,
but it was pitch black.
I didn't know where my squad was.
I didn't know where anything was,
and wasn't running around
to find out.
The shooting was getting worse.
I didn't want guys thinking I was the enemy.

They had us in a bowl
and were peppering the hell out of us
with 50 caliber machine guns
and mortars.

I took off my helmet
and started digging a hole
using my helmet as a shovel
to get below the field of flying shrapnel,
red hot and whistling
all around us.
I dug deep enough
to get the torso of my body
barely below the ground.

Guys were screaming for help.
One guy not too far away
had his arm blown off.

I laid on my back
and looked up at the sky full of stars,
red shrapnel and bluish-green tracers
flying and buzzing all around.
I listened to people screaming
and guys with authority calling out orders.
I thought, "What the hell!"

We called in naval gunfire
to bombard the enemy,
and the battle ended by daylight.

Listening Post

Our platoon of 35 men
were put on choppers
and taken to this remote place
on a hill above the jungle.
It was rocky with low grass
where we set up a perimeter.

The day was quiet with no fighting.
Nighttime, two of us
and my squad leader,
who was a black guy,
were ordered to go out on a listening post
halfway between the jungle
and our perimeter position.

The three of us
had been through a lot of fighting,
death, and rough situations.
We were battle-hardened and seasoned.

Two guys would sleep
while one guy kept watch.
We took turns throughout the night.

I was lying there
and felt my pantleg being tugged on.
The guy's name was Larry Boyer.
He shook me and whispered,
"I hear something."

Our squad leader was sleeping too.
I woke him up.
We got real alert,
grabbed our rifles,
and were ready
for whatever we might have to do.
All three of us could hear the enemy
walking through us.

In order to get to our line
and signal to the Marines we were coming,
our squad leader popped a five-star cluster flare.

An enemy soldier stood four feet away
with more all around.
The bright flare
scared the living shit out of them.
We ran like hell,
shooting behind us.

In the light of the flare
they saw there were only three of us,
and decided to chase us down.

We were hollering at our guys,
"Don't shoot!"
We reached the perimeter.
I forget what we called ourselves
out on a listening post,
so our guys knew
to let us through.
We yelled, "The enemy's coming!"

The enemy ran right into a nest
of M-60 machine guns.
Our guys opened up
and smoked them.
It turned into a hell of a gun battle,
almost hand to hand combat,
because some of them ran into our perimeter.

It was still dark
when the battle ended,
but we could hear moaning from their wounded.
None of our guys got hit.

Blood Trails

Daylight came.
There were several dead soldiers
lying around,
and blood trails everywhere
going back down into the jungle.

They'd left a machine gun
and two AK 47 assault rifles.
We made sure
the machine gun wasn't mined.
It was quite an honor
to capture a machine gun.

The enemy liked to take their dead.
They didn't want us to see their bodies.
It was one of their tactics.
They had big hooks
attached to ropes like fish hooks.
They'd jam that hook in a body,
a couple guys grabbed the rope
and towed it away.

We cleaned up the remaining bodies
and followed several blood trails
to track down wounded soldiers.
They were all North Vietnamese Army.

A special team
was in charge of dealing
with wounded enemy soldiers.

The Skull

Twenty-four hours later,
I was still on patrol
hunting for the wounded.

We were walking in this rocky little creek bottom
running down into the jungle.
Streams were the only way
you could navigate the jungle.

The jungle grew in layers,
one on top of the other.
It was so thick in spots,
you couldn't see the sky.
It was like going through a cave.

I was point man,
and walked up
on this dead North Vietnamese soldier
lying on the rocks
next to the stream.
He had died the night before
and was totally devoured by insects
in that short time.
Every lick of flesh was eaten off him
within 24 hours.
That's how vicious the jungle was.

I walked up to him.
His hair was still attached to the skull.
His hands sticking out of his shirt
were finger bones.

I gently kicked his head
and it rolled down the rocks.
I picked it up like a souvenir
and carried it around for a while.

Finally, it got too gruesome
for the lieutenant.

The Rockpile Encounter

There was an odd natural rock formation
right in the middle of the lowlands
and a valley of elephant grass
located a few miles
from the DMZ near Laos.
It reminded me of a giant thumb sticking up.
The cliff was 90 degrees in places.

On top of this rockpile
American troops made an observation post
to watch the Ho Chi Minh Trail.
They had a good view.

There was a platform
for landing helicopters,
and Special Forces rotated in and out.

A mile or two away
we were fighting in a triple-canopy jungle.

We received a report
the observation post
needed a squad at the bottom of the Rockpile
to check for enemy activity.
They were hearing things at night,
and would throw grenades down
the side of the mountain
to make sure the enemy wasn't sneaking up on them.
They'd never been shot at,
but could hear activity.

My squad took volunteers.
If you didn't volunteer
you went anyway,
and I got elected to go.

We started climbing up on vines
a foot in diameter.
It was like climbing a ladder.
Then we scaled big rocks.

Somebody started throwing boulders at us.
Some were bigger than basketballs
bouncing down
and crashing around us.
If you'd gotten hit with one
it could've done serious damage
or killed you.
We couldn't see
where they were coming from.

We called the base and said,
"They're throwing boulders at us!"
The answer was,
"They must be out of ammunition."

I was agile
and could climb fast,
so I was the first man going up.
I saw a boulder coming through the brush,
and dodged out of the way
before it crashed down past me.

I stood still
looking straight up the mountain
with my rifle pointed in the direction
the boulder came from.
I saw a brown flash.
Something was odd.
I climbed a little farther
and spotted an ape.
Monkeys had been throwing boulders at us.

We called back to the rear base
and told the Colonel,
"Sir, monkeys are throwing boulders at us.
We saw them."

It turned out to be a big joke,
being attacked by monkeys.
The locals called them "Rock Apes."

Thieves

Another kind of monkey
in the lower lands
would sneak into our camps at night
and steal our gear.

We had shiny Korean War
and World War II mess kits,
and shiny canteens.
The monkeys would grab anything shiny.

You couldn't hear them.
You'd see a shiny object
going away from you in the dark,
and think it was the enemy.

Somebody shot one,
and it was a monkey
the size of a 30-pound dog.

A Mass Grave

Thirty-five of us got transferred
to another area
around the Rockpile.
We were ordered
to go way down into the middle of the jungle.

We tried to get off the creek bottom
to avoid booby traps,
but we couldn't hack through the growth.
I had the only machete.
I'd written my father that I needed one,
and he'd sent it.

There was no way to cut through,
so we followed the river bottom cautiously.

Deep down in the jungle
we found a base camp
the enemy had just left.
They had huts and an ammunition dump.
Everything was cleaned out,
but the fire
where they'd cooked their food
was still warm.

There was a big cultivated round spot
50 by 50 feet in diameter.
It was a mass grave
where the enemy had buried their men.

We called back to the rear area
to some general or whoever,
and told him
we'd found a massive grave.
Headquarters gave us orders to uncover it
and make a body count.

We tried.
After digging a foot down
the stench of the bodies
was so putrid
we couldn't humanly do it.

Our lieutenant in charge called back
and said, "Look, this is bad.
The smell is horrid.
My men can't do this."
The answer was, "It doesn't matter.
We want a body count."

We tried again.
Guys were puking and gaging.
One guy reached down and grabbed a hand
and the skin started coming off.

After more puking
the lieutenant realized
we were getting nowhere.
He lied and told the general we'd dug it up
and there were 120 bodies.
We left that horrible place.

The whole war
was predicated around body counts.
Every dead body was counted.
I think we even counted animals.
It was ridiculous.

Wounded

There were bigger mountains
than the Rockpile,
but it stood out.
Photos on computers don't do it justice.

We'd spotted
a battalion of the enemy nearby,
and circled them in the jungle.
It wasn't a tight circle.
It was miles and miles around
in a triple canopy jungle,
real dense.

We were a blocking force
and the enemy kept probing us.
The North Vietnamese Army had been surrounded
for about two weeks
in this huge jungle.

Our naval gunfire had been hitting them hard
with artillery and mortars.
It was a big operation.
They had to break through us
and get to the Laotian border
for safety.

We'd been having encounters with them,
but the main force hadn't tried
to break through us yet.

We were all dug in at positions
with lots of ammunition.
My fox or fighting hole
had a 12 gauge Winchester shotgun,
a case of double ought buck shot,
and an M-14 with a couple thousand rounds.
The squad leader was with me
and he had a 45 pistol.

In front of our position
were claymore mines
all set up.

Because of the intense heat
and the direct sunlight
bearing down on us,
we put poncho shelters over these positions.

Our intelligence let us know
the night they were going to attack
to try to escape.

Our position was on a ridge,
and their position was on another ridge
almost a mile away.
Between us was the jungle.

I was down using the latrine trenches
at 6 p.m.
when they opened up on us
with machine guns and mortars
from their ridge.

I was lucky
I was going to the bathroom.
They almost hit my position directly.
The position next to me got hit.
Three or four guys were killed
and a couple mangled up bad.

As I was running back to my fighting hole
a mortar hit 30 feet from me.
I caught shrapnel
in my left hand,
and the blast knocked me down.
The concussion rattled my whole body
and messed my head up.
It took me a little while to recalibrate.

By the time I got back to my position
the enemy had quit.
My squad leader and I
got our fighting hole and ammunition
all back together.
He was a short-timer,
a black guy with a family back home,
with about three weeks left to serve,
a real nice guy.
The poncho that was our shelter
was blown all to hell.

There wasn't any more action
until 2 o'clock in the morning.
You could hear their bugles blowing,
one group of North Vietnamese Army signaling
to the others that it was time to advance.
Those bugles were scary as hell
and sent shivers down your spine.
It's like your life is very close
to being over.
It's a hard spot to be in.

They started coming through the jungle
towards us.
We saw their muzzle flashes
in the middle of the night,
and we opened up on them.

My squad leader stayed in the bottom
of the hole and reloaded.
I did the shooting.
I'd shoot the shotgun five times
and hand it to him.
He'd hand me the M-14. I'd shoot that,
then fire the claymores off.

I had come down with a fever
and didn't feel good at all.
I had a chunk of shrapnel in my hand,
but it wasn't a big piece
or bad enough to be evacuated
out of there.
My hand swelled way up.

After the battle ended
there was a lot of sporadic combat
that finally tailed off.

There were eight dead NVA soldiers
in front of our position.
I didn't know if it was me who shot them.
It could have been the machine gun
next to us.
So they weren't my confirmed kills,
but probable.
Plus they were enemy combatants.
They all had AK-47s
and were armed to the teeth,
and we were doing battle.
You didn't take their deaths personally.

Sick

Operation Hastings was a huge battle.
We had a lot of fighting
almost every day for two weeks,
and a lot of casualties.
Guys were being shipped out
and we were short of men.

The walking wounded
had to stay in position
as long as you could
get around and pull a trigger.

Towards the end of the operation
my fever started getting worse.
The shard of shrapnel
in my left hand
was lodged deep.
The corpsman tried to get it out,
but the wound started bleeding bad.

He decided to wait
till we got back to the rear
before I got it fixed.
He bandaged my hand up
and told me to live with it.

I was getting sicker.
I thought an infection in my hand
that was swelling up
was causing my fever,
so I dealt with it.
I was worried
about having my hand amputated.

I started becoming delirious.
Malaria is a strange thing.
You can have a temperature of 105 degrees
and you're freezing to death.
I was trying to find
anything to wrap myself in.
The temperature outside was 100,
and I was trying to get warm.

Finally, Operation Hastings ended
and we all got back to a rear base
near the DMZ.
I was so out of my head
I don't remember where it was.
There was a flat strip of land
like a road or an air base.

There was a big formation.
We were all standing
and I was up front.
Officers were going down the line
handing out medals.
I just keeled over and passed out.

Malaria

I don't know where I caught malaria.
Maybe it was drinking bad water
from the bomb crater,
or a lot of places.
It could've been the tree leeches
or swarms of mosquitoes.
All three of those carry malaria.

I remember
being on a medevac C-130 transport plane
carrying a bunch of wounded Marines.
Then I conked out.

I woke up a couple days later
in a tub of ice
in a medevac ward
in a big Army tent.

Corpsmen were trying to break my fever.
That bathtub full of ice
was pure hell,
one of the most horrible experiences
I've ever had in my life.

Corpsmen would carry me back to my cot
and I'd lay there with a high temperature,
freezing.
I'd put a blanket over me,
and they'd take it off.

They told me if I put the blanket back on
I'd have to go back in a tub of ice.
I swear to God,
I would've taken a bullet
rather than go back into that ice.

I was there a few days,
then got transferred
to a regular hospital in Da Nang.
I have no idea
where that tent hospital was.

The Hospital

Da Nang was a nice hospital
with comfortable beds.
I was in a place like a barracks
with maybe 20 patients.
It was clean with white sheets
and good food.
I was bedridden
for another ten days.

After three days I could get up,
walk around,
go to the bathroom,
and get food to eat.
But I'd get so weak
I had to go back to bed.

After a while I could get around
and go out of the hospital.
I wasn't able to drink,
but there was a club
with good entertainment.
Showgirls and comedians would show up.

I ate three good meals a day
and took medicine twice a day.
I was on my feet two weeks
before I left.

Bad Shape

A couple weeks after Hastings,
the first part of August,
I was still in the hospital
with malaria.

A Navy doctor came along
between the beds
with a colonel
who was giving out Purple Hearts.

They got to me
and the doctor was checking me out.
I was skinny,
in bad shape.
I'd only been there a couple days.

He saw these marks all over my body,
over 100 of them.
"What are those marks from?"
he asked.
I told him,
"That's from where we got bit up by leeches,"
and told them the story.

The doctor was a naval officer.
He put his head down
on the bed
and started weeping.
The Marine Colonel had a look on his face
like he'd seen a ghost.

They couldn't
get that out of their heads,
someone being attacked
by leeches.

Intensive Care Unit

The hospital asked for volunteers
to do different projects.
I wanted to do something
instead of just resting.
Nobody said, "Hey, you've got to do this."
I didn't know what I was getting into.

I went down to the ICU
where guys were in bad shape.

I walked in there...
It was horrible, horrible, horrible.
Terribly wounded guys were stacked up
with a number of tubes
coming out of them.
Very few were conscious.

Men were missing legs and arms
and some were burned.
The hospital had a burn unit.

The whole place smelled.
Bloody sheets laid all over the floor.
The ICU didn't seem kept up,
Three Vietnamese nurses
with grim looks on their faces
were changing IVs
and bandages.
I didn't see an American nurse at all.

The scene was so horrible
my mind went blank.
I forget what I did to help,
and didn't go to the ICU again.

Emergency Landing Zone

They needed help on the landing zone
where medevac choppers came in,
so I volunteered.
That was a hellacious job too,
a different intense emergency care.

Wounded guys came in screaming.
You'd lift them from that helicopter
onto a gurney
and rush them
into the emergency ward.
I was seeing wounded soldiers up close
while helping carry them.

Some guys' limbs would be dangling
by a piece of skin,
and some were dead.
You'd lay the dead on the tarmac
for Grave Registration to pick them up.

The slippery floors of the choppers
were covered with blood and body fluids,
maybe part of a blown off leg or arm.
All this had to be cleaned out.

Medevac choppers had coal shovels
lashed to their bulkheads.
They had to get in and out quick.
During a battle,
they'd make several runs back and forth.

Instead of swabbing the floors,
the crew chief used the shovel
to scoop limbs, body fluids and blood
out on the tarmac.
Volunteers cleaned it up
after the chopper took off.

You'd slip and slide around.
It was a gruesome job.

Ambush

I healed up and went back to my unit
in this hellacious place.
We were supposed to be protecting
a friendly village.

We had a perimeter around this schoolhouse
where our command was.
Our outposts were 100 yards out
and far apart.

We weren't very well protected.
The enemy could've run us over,
but it was supposed to be
a friendly place,
and we got along with the people.

Their troops called Popular Forces
came in with us,
and joined us on patrols.

The trouble started out slowly.
At first just sniper shots
into our compound every night.
Then we'd go out on patrol
and come back with wounded,
or we'd go out and get somebody killed.
It just escalated.

I was a team leader by then,
advancing up
to become squad leader.
Sometimes I'd take the whole squad out,
but most times I had three guys.

Pfc. Martinez was one of the first guys from the States
to join my team.
He could hardly speak English,
but we got to where we could communicate
with one another.
He was a good warrior.

We fought in battles together.
In fact we fought
in the Battle of Hastings together.

For some reason
Martinez was transferred to the Third Squad.
I was in the First.

We were out on patrol
between two graveyards
when the enemy ambushed the rear squad.
My squad was in the middle of a field,
dead ass out in the open,
easy pickings
if the enemy had been in the right spot.

I looked back at the lieutenant.
He waved and yelled,
"Move it out! Move it out!"
We didn't know what had happened yet.

We reached the other graveyard
and sat there listening
to the battle going on.

After it calmed down
one of my guys said,
"I'm going back across the field
and check out what happened."
"Okay, go ahead."

Cpl. Perez was a seasoned Marine
and he came back crying.
I said, "Perez, what happened?"
He answered, "The rear squad got wiped out.
So and so was dead.
So and so was dead.
So and so was wounded."
One of the dead was Martinez.

A chopper came in and picked up the wounded.
The enemy saw Perez
running back across that field. A group of them
decided to try and catch him.
They got real close,
six to ten feet away in their advance
to our position,
and we hadn't heard or seen them.

It was daytime.
We were on the corner of two fields
in among the graves.

An explosion went off
between me and another guy.
The concussion was close and
rang my bell.
I was hurt.
My brain was scrambled temporarily.

This enemy soldier jumped on top of a grave
and pointed his rifle at me.
I was conscious enough to know I was dead.
A bunch of my friends had just been killed,
and this guy was going to kill me.
All these thoughts
were going through my head.

I couldn't pick up my rifle
to defend myself.
Perez shot and killed the guy
before he killed me.
Thirty seconds later I came to my senses
and started doing battle.

The Pilot

A spotter plane like a piper cub
with a Marine pilot
came in, flying straight at us,
and fired a rocket.
A big ball of flame blew up
30 yards away.

A spotter plane carried four rockets
of white phosphorous.
They were deadly
and if a rocket hit near you
it could burn you alive,
but mainly it made a lot of smoke.

The enemy was screaming
and we panicked.
We didn't know what the hell to do
if he was shooting at us.

We ran to the edge of the graveyard
and the field.
I waved my arms
to show the pilot I was a Marine.
He shot another rocket
five feet over my head
at the enemy.

What happened is
he'd spotted the enemy right on us.

He shot all four rockets,
swung around,
banked his plane,
hung out the window with an M-16 rifle
and started shooting.

He had a long handlebar mustache.
He was so close
we could see him plain as day.
I could kiss that man.
He got the enemy off our backs.

Pfc. Martinez

Back at our compound
they'd picked up all of our dead
except Martinez.

They brought him in on an Amtrac,
a tank vehicle that can go in water.

They pulled up
near my position,
and unloaded him.

I walked over to say good-bye.
He was shot up pretty bad.
His one leg had a compound fracture
with the bone sticking out.
I got my air mattress
and put it on him
and covered him up with my poncho.

A chopper came in
to get Martinez,
and blew the poncho off.

L/cpl. Starcher

This guy named Starcher was in my squad
under my charge.
He was an "FNG,"
a college boy, an athlete
whose girlfriend was Miss Virginia.
He didn't belong in Vietnam.

Starcher was well-spoken,
and a real handsome guy.
I thought, "Man, I hope he makes it."

I'd been out in the field a long time,
and drew some light duty.
I got a chance to take a prisoner
on a truck back to Da Nang.

I delivered the prisoner
and came back to regimental headquarters.
There was a score sheet on the wall
of KIA or WIA,
killed in action or wounded in action.
It was a big chalk board
of all causalities
and information on the squads too,
guys that were still alive.

The board listed my name and squad.
I saw Starcher's name as KIA.
"What the hell?"

"Yes, Starcher was killed yesterday."
I couldn't believe it.
He was riding on top of an Amtrac
in a prone position
when the squad came under fire.

Nobody even knew he was dead
until they bailed out
and yelled, "Let's go Starcher!"
He'd been shot
right through the top of his head.

First Confirmed Kill

We stayed inside this little perimeter
where the kids came in.
We had no security or barbed wire,
just remote lookout posts
guarded by two or three guys
who could hardly see each other.
The enemy could've run us over
at any time.

There was a man with a water buffalo
plowing this little rice paddy
in the center of our perimeter.
I knew this guy
because I'd been there before.
I told him if he'd let me plow
with his water buffalo
I'd give him a cigar.

He agreed
and harnessed me up to his animal.
Other guys were standing around
laughing like hell
at Lelito plowing with a buffalo.
I gave him a cigar
and we were both smoking.
That was a fun day.

Every night we got shot at; two or three rounds.
We couldn't figure it out.
The shooter couldn't hit anything,
but he shot at us every night.

A day after I was playing with the buffalo
we got in a fire fight,
a full-blown battle
with machine guns firing.

About 300 yards away
this guy was walking across a rice paddy.
He was carrying a rifle
and something about him
didn't look right.
My squad leader said, "Lelito, shoot him!"

I picked up my M-14,
beaded in on him
and missed the first shot.
At 300 yards I couldn't see him very well.
With the second shot he went down.

After the battle
we went out to retrieve the body.
At the first dike there was nothing.
In the fog of battle
you can't determine the exact location.
It's like shooting a deer.
You think it was closer,
but it was farther out.

We walked over to the next dike
and there was the guy I'd smoked a cigar with
deader than a doornail.
I'd shot him right in the neck.
Turned out the guy
with the water buffalo
had been shooting at us.

The Vietcong gave him this old antique rifle
that came from the French
out of some war in Europe.
It was a bolt action with a busted stock
that he'd used.

The Vietcong probably gave him ammunition
and threatened him,
that if they didn't see three empty cartridges
every day,
they were going to kill him and his whole family.
So he had to do it.

It really hit me hard.
I found a photograph in his pocket
of his wife and kids.
I can still see those faces
clear as today.
I felt like I lost a piece of myself
and wanted it back.

Lelito's team home, or "hooch," September and October 1966. The grass walls offered no protection from the enemy and, during the rainy season, would flood chest-high. On most days, the hooch took hostile fire.

Lelito's first sniper rifle, an M-1 Garand. Although it was a remnant of WW II, it had an excellent scope and shot accurately at 600 yards.

Numb

A week and a half before Christmas
we got into a heavy battle
with a large force.

My squad leader, Sgt. Ortega, was killed
right next to me.
He was shot in the head
and died instantly.

We'd done battle together
and he'd saved my life
several times.

It was a numbing experience,
but I didn't let my emotions get involved.
That's dangerous.
Your senses are down.

You have to be vigilant at all times
in chaotic situations like that.
So I continued on.

Six of us carried him on a poncho
throughout the night,
and got back to the rear.

We found out
there was an enemy sniper
with a silencer on his weapon.
He'd just gun guys down.
We couldn't hear or see him.

Later on I was guiding a group of tanks
out to this area.
One of our guys, sitting on top of a turret,
spotted the sniper
and shot and killed him.

The Buddha Statue

The Vietcong liked to fight in graveyards
where we'd pursue them.
The graves were mounds
four or five feet high,
a few feet apart,
and covered with grass on top
another couple feet high.

They could get up there
and see us coming
from a long ways away
traversing through the mounds.

They would ambush us in these graveyards
that were centuries old.

There were tombs
every hundred acres or so,
for important people
like village chiefs or generals.

The tombs were built of concrete
ten feet wide and twelve feet long
with tile roofs
and a door on one end.

If you opened the door
and went in,
there was a burial vault
in the middle of a concrete
floor where the body was.

In the corner was an altar
with a little statue of Buddha,
and a bowl of rice or sand
with sticks of incense.
There was a vase they'd put flowers in,
and knick-knacks
or little cups
that reminded me of marbles.

Guys might think that stuff was junk,
but it had to do with their religion.
It was sacred.

We used these tombs
for places of safe refuge.
If you were in there
the Vietcong wouldn't shoot at it,
throw a grenade or satchel charge
through the door,
or fire a rocket at you.

If it was raining
one squad could fit inside.
These old tombs
weren't kept up very well.
The gifts on the altar
hadn't been used in a long time.

There were spider webs
with moss growing on the walls.
Inside was gnarly and scary,
especially if you were in a storm.
The lightning would flash,
and you could see the expressions
of the other guys' faces;
but you felt safe.

One morning this guy grabbed a six-inch Buddha
off the altar,
stuffed it in his pack,
and off we went.
I didn't even see him do it.

Back at our base, at the post office,
he packaged it up
and sent it home to his girlfriend.
I found out what happened later.

Soon as the Buddha arrived
at the girl's house,
her mother opened the package
and looked at the statue.
She was there by herself.

She sat the Buddha on the fireplace mantle,
and walked into the kitchen
to start dinner.
Grabbed a knife
to open a package of meat,
and sliced a big gash in her hand.
She had to get stitches.

While the mother was at the doctor's,
another family member
got in a bad car accident
and was busted up.
A string of horrendous bad luck
continued for days.

The family got to thinking
it all started when that Buddha came
to the house.
They needed to get that Buddha
back to Vietnam
and back in that tomb.

They contacted their Congressman
and told him the story.
He ordered the Buddha to be sent home
soon as possible.
How it got from the States to Vietnam
I don't know.

We'd moved to a different location.
A helicopter came in
and the pilot told us we had orders
to go back to that cemetery
and put a Buddha
back in a tomb.
He handed the little statue
to the guy who stole it.

I didn't know the story.
I thought the order was stupid,
and wanted to chuck it.
The helicopter landed us a couple miles
from the area.
You couldn't land in the cemetery
with all those mounds.
A small squad of us
had to go on patrol
through this dangerous place
to haul that little Buddha back
to its tomb.

The guy who stole it
had to go with us,
and he carried it.

The Vietcong Knew

The Vietcong knew everything,
what kind of food we ate,
when we'd come and go.
They even knew our names.

Kids would infiltrate our posts.
We'd let them in
because they brought us delicious fresh bread
the French had taught them how to make.
They'd bring us ice.
I don't know where they got it.

They'd go back
and the Vietcong would question them
about us.
These kids were ten to twelve years old,
and that was their job.
"If you don't tell us
we'll kill your family."

Then mamasan would come in.
It was a luxury for us
to have our clothes washed.
We had no way to wash them.
So she would go back
and tell the Vietcong what she knew.

Later, I had a bounty on my head
because of my success as a sniper
and other things that happened.
The Vietcong knew about me
from talk.
Guys would leak information
in the villages, not knowingly.

The Outpost

I left infantry Line Company for a sniper platoon.
When I wasn't out on a mission
I stayed at regimental headquarters
resting.

Three miles from our position
was an outpost of Marines.

It had apparently been there a long time
guarding a Catholic church.
The perimeter was coils of concertina wire,
razor sharp,
and sandbag bunkers,
with our soldiers' cots inside.

Civilians would come and go.
Marines could get haircuts by the Vietnamese
and buy pot or whatever.

I went to the outpost to visit
a buddy who got transferred there.
They were living large
listening to rock 'n' roll and Motown music
blaring all the time.
I couldn't believe what I was seeing.

I told my friend, "Man,
you guys are going to get smoked
some night.
You're going to get hit,
letting all these civilians come and go.
The Vietcong's got you pinned."

"Na," he said. "We're secure.
The regiment is only three miles away."

I was back at regiment headquarters
one night.
Sure enough,
we started hearing explosions going off at the outpost.

The enemy had sent in sappers.
A sapper has nothing but a satchel
carrying a block of explosives.
You pull a pin and a fuse starts.
Within six seconds
a huge explosion goes off.
Sappers hit every one of those bunkers.

We captured one sapper
and found out what happened.

Vietcong spies made drawings
of the outpost.
They built a model up in the mountains,
and practiced attacking it
for two months.

While our guys were smoking dope
and listening to Motown or The Doors,
the sappers snuck in
and blew them all to hell.

After the enemy overran the place
we got called to go there and clean up
the mess.
It was the most horrific scene.
We picked up bodies in body bags,
and parts of bodies.
You'd find a guy's clothes bloody and shredded
with not much left of him.

My buddy got hit good.
I walked out of his bunker
and picked up his boot.
His foot and ankle were still in it.

Christmas Present

It was Christmas 1966.
There was a Bob Hope show,
but one squad had to go out on patrol.
Our group drew the short straw.

It was a cease fire.
We'd made an agreement with the enemy
that there'd be no action
for two days.
I didn't believe that at all.

On patrol we had to be cautious.
You could get ambushed
at any time.
We traveled jungle areas
along a river,
and across open rice paddies.
There was no other way.

Separating rice paddies
are dikes
also used for trails.
In the middle were little islands
that offered cover.

It was Christmas,
dusk turning to dark.
We split up into three groups.
I took my team across first,
and nothing happened.

The second team was coming across
when they got hit.
I could see the green tracer bullets
going right at our men,
and the enemies' muzzle flashes.

Two of our men were shot
and fell off the lee side of the dike.
I could hear them hollering
for a corpsman
who was still in the rear.

We opened up on the enemies' muzzle flashes.
I sneaked back
where the wounded guys were.

The enemy was still hammering at us,
tearing the dike apart
with gunfire.

We kept calling for help on the radio,
but everybody was at the Bob Hope Show
watching Nancy Sinatra.

I was in neck-deep rice paddy water
pinned against the dike for protection
with seriously injured men.
Finally, we dragged the wounded on ponchos
to the island.

We picked up a stray helicopter
on the radio
delivering pizzas to the Army.
I told them about our trouble,
and to be prepared to come in hot,
which meant they were going to be shot at.

The wounded were loaded
on the pizza chopper,
and we made it back to our command post.

Our guys were coming
back all whooped up
from watching pretty girls
and drinking lots of beer.
They were all cleaned up.

I was sitting in our sandbag bunker,
covered in mud and another man's blood.
I was numb.

They had a bunch of Christmas gifts
from the States.
One guy gave me a present.
I thought it was a box of canned peaches.
In Vietnam peaches were like nectar from heaven
and tasted so good.

I opened the gift up.
It was dog food,
with an insulting note
from a college student back home.
It said, "Chow down, Animal!"

Dog Food and Protests

Until the dog food present
I was fighting for my country,
to stop the advance of communists,
and the domino effect
all over southeast Asia.

As a kid, I fell into that way of thinking.
During the Cold War,
in school we practiced hiding under
our desks
in case of a nuclear bomb attack.

I got a raw feeling
over that dog food gift,
trying to sort out why
someone would do that.

I didn't know there was protesting back home.
Never heard about it.
We were always out in the bush.

Over the next few weeks, "FNG's,"
f---ing new guys,
would join us.

I started asking them
about this protesting business
back home.
I realized our country was divided
about what was going on here,
almost to the point of violence.
There was a civil war
in our own country.

After that I wasn't fighting
for a patriotic idea anymore.
For the six or seven months I had left
I started fighting for survival.
I just wanted to get home.

Sniper Training

At the hospital back in Da Nang
the guy in the bed next to me
was a warrant officer
who'd been in World War II, Korea,
and, now, Vietnam.

We were talking
about what was going on,
because he hadn't been there very long.
I told him the situation.

He asked, "Do you have any snipers
in your outfit?"
"No."

He'd been a sniper during the Korean War.
He told me,
"When you get back to your outfit,
I'm going to call for you."

After I went back to my outfit,
he called my commanding officer
and asked if I would consider
going to three days of sniper training.

I thought, "Man,
I'm not going to be eaten up
by bloodsuckers.
I'll have a hot meal every night.
Yes, I'm going to do that."

He called five of us back,
trained us,
and gave each of us a sniper rifle,
a World War II M-1 Garand
with a side-mounted four-
power scope,
a very accurate rifle,
but it was heavy.
Later on we got more sophisticated weaponry.

I'd been with my line company seven months.
I was with a sniper unit eight months.

The Course

Sniper training
was an experimental course
to see if snipers could be effective
in the rough jungle conditions
of Vietnam.

Our instructor, S/Sgt. Carlos Hathcock,
was a Marine Corps legend
with over 90 kills,
but I didn't know that at the time.

After three days
we returned to our units.

Because of our success
the 1st Marine Regiment
constructed a 1000-yard range
and selected 30 Marines
from various units
to make up and train
the 1st Marine Scout Sniper Unit.

After two weeks
of extensive long-range shooting instruction,
to qualify you had to shoot ten rounds
at a 22-inch target,
and hit all your shots at 1000 yards.

We used a new, souped-up
Remington Model 700 308
bolt action rifle
with a 3" by 9" scope.

If you didn't qualify
you were sent back to a line unit.

After qualification
we were sent back to Regiment
for deployment to any unit
that needed a sniper.

Lelito on Highway 1 outside of Da Nang, hooking a ride to to his unit 20 miles North.

True Hard —125

Scout Sniper

To go off as a sniper
I felt would be easier.

When I was chosen,
I took it.
I didn't like being in firefights
with the responsibility
of other people's lives at stake.

A sniper turned out
to have a lot more responsibility.
Sometimes you were in charge
of large groups of men.

You had to be good with maps,
be a scout
and take these groups
into an area
where the outfit had never been before.
You'd be responsible
for maybe 50 men.

It got a little hairy out there.
It was not an easy job.

What I liked about it was
I thought that I wouldn't have
to be out in the field
all the time
but it didn't turn out that way.

Sniper

Being a sniper
compared to a regular soldier
was a lot of boredom.
You might sit
four or five nights and days
in a dangerous place by yourself.

You'd try to keep yourself clean.
You were concerned
and didn't sleep much.
There were five-minute catnaps
and you'd wake up.

Then it got intense.
The time came
when you encountered your enemy.
How you handled that by yourself
was a trying moment.

You may not have wanted to kill your enemy.
It depended on how many there were.

If there was a squad or platoon
or even more
coming across an open field,
you'd observe them all
and figure out
which one was the highest-ranking leader.

You'd watch hand signals,
look at the way they were dressed,
the weapons they had.
A high-ranking person
usually wore just a pistol
and didn't carry a rifle.
Behind him was a radio man.

You wanted to disable the leader,
not kill him.
You wanted him to be in agony
and scream real loud.

That would confuse the rest of them,
and give you time
to call in gunfire from a gunship.

You'd fire one shot. That was your job,
not sitting there shooting as many people
as you could.

If you fired more than once
they'd figure out where you were
firing from,
and catch you.

Revenge

I'd changed before Martinez's death.
After my squad leader was killed,
I saw an advantage for revenge
if I became a sniper,
and I took it.

Vietnam was a rough place.
I'd experienced all the battles in infantry
with Hotel Company.
Then got transferred to Sniper Platoon,
and sent out with other units.

I made ten kills
the first operation I went on
right out of sniper school.

I was assigned to a company
of 150 or 200 men
with a battalion.
I had a group around me
and was heavily guarded.
They pushed the enemy into me,
and I shot them
one after another.

I'd had kills before that
and was seasoned and trained.
That gave me a reputation
I didn't want.
When people needed somebody
it got to be, "Send Lelito."
I was always out in the field.

I was 20 years old
and had the highest number of kills
in our sniper platoon
when I was discharged
out of Vietnam.

When not on a mission, Lelito carried a 12 gauge shotgun. The assault rifle on the sandbag (lower right) was recovered from a Viet Cong soldier.

The Shot

When you took that shot
you wanted the bullet
to go where it was supposed to.

You had to know your limitations
and your rifle's.
If your rifle was zeroed in at 400 yards,
a precision shooter was very accurate
out to 800 yards.
At 900 yards, a 308 bullet drops
below the speed of sound,
begins to wobble,
and accuracy becomes impaired.
At 1200 yards
the bullet drops 55 feet.

Most of the field shooting
beyond 600 yards was holdover,
no more than an estimate.
In field conditions hitting a target
at 1000 yards was remarkable.
Carlos Hathcock had told us,
"Taking a 'SWAG,'
a scientific wild ass guess,
could cost you your life."

You looked through that high-powered scope
and had to read the weather.
There was a lot to do.
You didn't just lay a rifle
on a sandbag
and shoot someone from a thousand yards.

In your scope
you could see heat waves
coming off the earth.
You read those heat waves.

You compiled windage
and all that information
in your mind.

You had to control your heartbeat
and breathing.

Your heart was going boom, boom, boom!
because you were excited
and in a real tight position.

You had to get your heart rate down.
You took two deep breaths.
On the third breath
you let it halfway out
and wait no longer than three seconds
to make your shot.
That was the steadiest you would be.
Then you squeezed the trigger
oh so gently,
because every little move
from your body was transmitted to your rifle.
Every shot was different.

Fight and Hurt

I'd been out for two days by myself
sitting in a position
in a low, hidden area.
You'd do anything to keep your mind active.
I watched two tarantulas fight.
I watched ants fight.

A line of ants came from one place.
Another line of different ants
came from another direction,
and they fought it out
right in front of me.

Everything in that country wanted to fight
and hurt each other.

The Little Boy

I got assigned to an Echo Company unit
as a sniper.
The Vietcong had destroyed a civilian village,
killed everybody in it
and burned the huts and houses.
The village had fraternized with us,
or had done something good
for the Americans.

We were on reconnaissance
to do a body count,
maybe make contact with the enemy
or gain information.

We hiked down this trail
five miles off the main road.
A mile from the village
we could smell the burnt flesh,
the bloated and dying bodies.
We dreaded what we were heading into.

Up on the point with my spotter
I saw the village,
and we walked past a couple burned houses.
I could see the dead bodies inside.

When someone burns to death
there's a fetal position
they almost always take
with their legs spread apart.
I've seen countless charred bodies,
so I know how they look.

On the trail ahead
I saw something white moving.
Everything else was still and dead.

I walked closer
and put my scope on the white motion.
It was a little boy around three years old
sitting on a dike
with something white behind him.

Up closer
I saw he was with his dead mother.
She was carrying a little pack
the size of a woman's purse
full of their belongings,
for trying to evacuate.
She'd been dead two or three days.

The little boy wasn't injured,
but he had an eye poked out
from sometime earlier.

I don't want to get into the gory details
of what the discussions were
to do with this kid.
I wasn't having any part of it.

"This boy is coming with us," I said.
I was a corporal with field rank
arguing with a lieutenant.

I wasn't a part of those guys.
I was attached to them.
They didn't even know me,
and didn't care about me
or my spotter.
The argument finally broke down,
and he agreed.

I said, "The next village we come to
we'll drop the boy off."
"Fine," he said, "but you're taking care of him."
My spotter agreed.
He was the guy who was always with me.

We reached this village
and the people were poorer than poor.
You don't know what poor is
until you've visited a country like Vietnam
in 1966.

I knew a little bit of their language
and would talk to a motherly looking lady.
She'd get a look of fear in her eyes
and run away.
They wouldn't take the kid.

I carried this little boy a couple days,
fed him and cared for his toilet needs.
He latched right on to me
and wouldn't leave my side.

The last night
I laid out a bed for him
with a poncho and jacket
next to me.
My spotter and I were on a listening post.
The other guys didn't want that kid
in their area.

I always slept with a 45 pistol on my chest
so I could jump into action quick
if I had to.
My rifle laid next to me,
but I had more firepower with a 45
than a bolt action rifle.

We were on a 50-50 watch.
My spotter shook my knee
and said, "Corporal Lelito, it's your turn."
He was standing up.

A terrible explosion went off.
I could feel every organ in my body shake.
My brain was screwed up.
The little boy was screaming
and my spotter was hollering.
He'd taken a big part of the blast
in the back of his legs and ass.

I could hear the enemy
rustling around in the dark
and talking.
They didn't realize
we were with a larger group.
They'd spotted us somehow
and threw a grenade in on us.

I got hit in the head above the eye
and blood was running down
my face.
I thought I'd lost my left eye
because I couldn't see out of it.
It was 4 o'clock in the morning.

The kid was still screaming.
I was trying to get him behind me,
and feeling down for my wounded man.
I put my hand right in the cheek of his ass.
He was hit bad.

I called for help.
A corpsman and two other guys came
and dragged us back to the command center.

We couldn't get a chopper in.
At night
we couldn't clear a landing zone.
So the corpsman patched us up.

After daylight
I didn't want to leave.
I wasn't wounded bad enough
and wanted to help finish this fight off.

They loaded my spotter on the chopper,
and I put the little boy on.
The last thing I saw
was this kid staring at my face with a terrified look
with his one eye missing.

I wish I would've thought to write a note
to send with him,
so later on in life
he could know what happened.

Snails

I was assigned to a recon unit
of the 1st Marines.
Helicopters dropped us into an area
up near the DMZ.
It was called a vertical assault.

From above,
the ground looked like a grassy field,
but it was tall elephant grass
ten feet high.

Jumping out of the backs of Chinooks
at that height
carrying full combat gear,
some guys broke their legs.

We were pinned down with our injured,
and the enemy started mortaring us.

My squad was ordered
to go find the mortar positions
and knock 'em out.
We chopped our way through the elephant grass
and did the job.

Back at the landing zone
our men were in a tough spot
with lots of wounded.
It felt like 120 degrees
and everybody was dehydrating.

They cleared a place
for our choppers to land,
and pulled everybody out,
leaving us behind.

They figured we could fend for ourselves,
which we did.
But we didn't have any supplies.
We'd left our packs where we'd jumped.
All we took were our rifles
and a couple canteens of water.

With no food
we ran out of water,
and had to seek the lowlands in the jungle
where there were creeks.

All this time
we were dodging the enemy.
The Vietcong used trails along those creeks.

We hid five or six days
going hungry along the edge of a creek,
 waiting for our guys to come back for us.

One guy passed out
from starvation or malaria.
We thought he was going to die.

I saw some good-sized snails
down in the water.
I figured, "The French eat snails,
we can too."
I reached down
and pulled some out.

I cracked open snails,
mushed them up in my mouth,
and spit them in this guy's mouth
to nourish him.

It brought him back to life.
We had a hard time
working our way out of there,
but were rescued
days later.

A Box Mine

There were only 30 of us snipers
to begin with.
After the first operation
it went down to 20.

Some didn't have the nerve
to pull the trigger
and kill a person.
They were mustered out,
and several were wounded.

After my spotter was wounded
and sent back to the States,
I got attached to a tank platoon.

I would guide the squad
into areas where I'd already been.
There were three tanks
and my name was scout-sniper.

We moved into a bad area
where we'd seen some action.

I was riding on the front fender of this tank,
with my legs dangling over the side.
I had my back pack on.
For some reason I changed positions.
I pulled my legs up and crossed them
Indian style with my rifle across my lap.

The tank hit a box mine.
I saw a wall of fire go up
in front of me
with parts of the tank's tracks
mingled in the flames.

I flew up through the air,
did a somersault,
hit the corner of the turret,
rolled off the tank
and fell on the other side.
I was knocked out for a few seconds.

When I came out of it
my clothes were smoldering
from catching fire.

I wondered if my legs were blown off.
I knew I had my hands,
because I was patting myself
to make sure
the fires on my clothes were out.
I could see.
All these thoughts were rushing
through my mind.
I got up on my feet
and was able to move around.
I realized I wasn't hurt
as bad as I was afraid I might be.

I was so glad to be alive
I didn't even tell anybody
about my aching wrist and ankle.
I didn't know until years later
that I'd gotten busted up.
I had two hairline fractures
but I figured I had two sprains.
I hobbled around,
did the best I could
and healed up.

Alone

If there was a chance
I might have a bunch of enemy coming across
my kill zone,
I had to be prepared
to radio in artillery or naval gunfire.
Sometimes I'd prepare the kill zone
by having the battery fire
a dud round.

A dud round
came in and kicked up dust.
It didn't make an explosion
that warned anybody.

I'd set my coordinates from that.
My guys might send a tank rumbling over
real quick,
or infantry in helicopters.

A lot of preparation
went into being a sniper,
because sometimes you were alone
or undermanned.

Hate

Every sniper I've ever known
had a heart,
but you learned to hate your enemy.

I don't care
if you were a rifleman in the infantry,
grenadier, or artilleryman,
you hated your enemy,
and your job was to kill them.

You were told to squeeze that trigger.
If you couldn't do that,
you didn't belong on the job.
Other people's lives were at stake.

If you ever got into that situation
your life changed forever.

A lot of guys that experienced it ...
when they got home,
they depended on alcohol
and different kinds of drugs
for self-medication.
It was the worst thing you could do.

I Just Can't

When I killed with a scope
I was seeing first-hand
the bullet's impact
on who I was shooting at.

You called your shot.
At 400 to 600 yards,
I could keep my bullet in a belt buckle.

You looked through your scope
as the rifle went off,
and saw that man
while the bullet was traveling.

You saw him wrench and a red mist come out
where the bullet was exiting.

Some sights were even worse.
I can't even talk about them.
I just can't.
I've skimmed over the story
if you can imagine.

Sergeant E-5

I went over to Vietnam as a private
and came back after fifteen months
a Sargeant E-5.
It was 1966-67.

The way I received rank
was by surviving
my time on the job.

They'd put me in a higher position
and with that position
I'd need the rank to go with it.

I was 20 years old,
didn't even shave,
and was a Sergeant E-5.

Guys had been in the service 20 years
trying to get that rank.

I was all over
the northern part of Vietnam,
all the way from the DMZ
to Da Nang
and in between—
from the Laotian border
to the South China Sea.

"Near the end of my tour in Vietnam, in late 1967, guarding the regimental headquarters."

Nightmares

I still have nightmares,
but not as extreme.

I dream that I've killed somebody,
and hide or bury them
so they won't be discovered.

People are getting closer and closer
to finding out
I killed this person.
You know you're going to get caught
by having it on your mind.
It's scary.

They say war is war,
but when you kill somebody
you take everything
that man was ever going to have.
It was said long before Clint Eastwood.

You lose too much.
You lose something that you can't get back,
and wish you could.
Maybe it's a part of your soul,
or all of your soul.

After the killing got easy
and didn't matter,
I began to wonder
what kind of person I was.

Every time I got on a helicopter
to meet up with reconnaissance
or whoever I was supposed to serve,
someone was going to die.
That's all there was to it.
I wasn't out there to play tiddlywinks.

I still dream these things,
or wake up in the middle of the night
and think about it.

Home

I got dumped off
at a base in San Francisco
on the shore of the Pacific Ocean.
I still smelled like gun powder and jungle
and had 300 bucks in my pocket.

We had to get shots.
They searched us thoroughly
to make sure we didn't have any contraband,
weapons, or dope.

After the shots
we went through a debriefing process
and a class.
They told us not to talk
about our experiences.
The next day we were released.

I got out of there at nighttime.
The place we were at
was on a high ridge
looking down at the city
with all the lights.

There was an American flag flying
on the base
with lights on it.
I'll never forget the feeling I had
looking at that flag,
knowing I was home
and safe.

I could eat what I wanted,
get all the water I wanted.
I didn't need to be armed.
Seeing that flag
meant all this to me.
It was a wonderful sight.

I took a cab to the airport
and bought a ticket to Traverse City.
My parents had moved
from the Detroit area
to a house on Lake Bellaire.
I'd never been there.
I hired a cab driver to take me to their house.

It was summertime in July
and my family didn't know I was coming.
They saw the cab pull into the drive
and me get out
and open the trunk
to get my duffle bag.
They came out and were happy.
I was happy to see them.

My sister was waitressing
in a little restaurant on Torch River,
so they took me to see her.
She was quite emotional.

I was on leave at home for a month
and spent a lot of time in Traverse City.
It was the first time
I'd ever been there.
It was a beautiful, peaceful place.

I'd sit on the beach on East Bay
off Four Mile Road,
looking over the water
and talking with people.

Nobody knew what Vietnam was.
There were only two TV channels
and one radio station
that went off the air at 8 o'clock.
If you couldn't pick up Chicago,
you didn't get music after 8 p.m.
That was okay by me.

Then I returned to the jungle of San Francisco
to finish my tour of duty.
That was completely chaotic.
You'd go down to Haight Ashbury District
and there'd be every kind of weirdo.

San Francisco

Everybody in the barracks had a top-secret clearance
and worked hard
guarding that top-secret base.
That's not a job they gave any guy.

They were spit-shined and armed four days on,
three days off
working 24-hour shifts,
on duty four hours
and off eight hours,
but always at the barracks.
I ran a pistol range,
was a rifle coach and instructor.
It was a grueling job.
If the shooting range was down
I went off base sometimes
and transferred bodies from Vietnam,
or picked up prisoners.

When it came time to go into San Francisco,
guys weren't prepared for that
with the problems we came back with
from the jungle and battles.

They'd been living like dogs.
Now guys were exposed to a big city environment
with alcohol, drugs,
women, and song,
any kind of entertainment you wanted.
San Francisco in the late 1960s
was happening.

It was wild.
Guys were digging life.
They all had cars.
I had a car and a motorcycle.
But we had hard times there.
A lot of guys were killed in car accidents
at high speeds.

Nobody figured they were going to live
very long,
so, "Hell, let's live it up!"

The nightlife was hard on us.
Guys were overdosing,
and drinking was a problem.
You could go into Chinatown
and get deep dark into gambling.

These guys—including myself—
came back from a terrible war,
and there was no help of any kind
for our mental condition.

If you needed psychological mentoring
from someone who knew
how to deal with combat stress,
you'd get a Section 11
which went down in your records.
Then you were a Shitbird.

But the American flag was flying.
You had all the food
you wanted to eat,
and all the water
you wanted to drink.
And you didn't have to run around with a gun
all the time.

Bedlam

I went through a living hell
living on that top-secret Naval base
before I got out of the service.

Things were chaotic.
Everybody was either drunk, stoned or fighting
at times.
It was bedlam.

Men would have anxiety attacks
in the morning
after long nights of drinking.

I was on duty for the barracks one night,
and heard a ruckus going on.
I ran upstairs
and this soldier was in the corner,
foaming at the mouth,
with a survival knife
slashing at anybody
who got near him.

He was having a drug attack
combined with Post Traumatic Stress,
and was hollering crazy stuff.

I had my 45 pistol
since I was on duty,
and was seriously thinking I might have to shoot him.
I didn't want to shoot
a fellow comrade,
but was ready to.

I got a group of guys together.
We grabbed a mattress,
charged, pinned him in a corner,
and disarmed him.

The MP's came with a straitjacket
and took him away.

A Soldier's Elegy for Martin Luther King, Jr.

After 13 months in Vietnam
I was stationed on a naval base
on a peninsula near San Francisco.
There were 35 thousand sailors,
with 83 Marines
guarding the place.
I was a Marine range officer and weapons instructor
teaching rifle lessons.

A lot of Marines were having a hard time
dealing with Post Traumatic Stress.
After a night on the town
soldiers were having drug-influenced
combat flashbacks.
It was not uncommon
to have guys brought back to the base
in straitjackets.

I never did drugs,
but I spent my time in the Frisco bars.
If I went off base,
I had to dress in civilian clothes.
If I wore my uniform
people treated me like a war criminal.

Half our barracks men were black
and half were white.
As a Sergeant E-5
I was the leader of the white guys.
Black guys were my friends too,
but we'd gang up
and didn't associate much back and forth.

The command was smart enough
to make the leader of the black guys
and I roommates.
Boonie was his nickname.
He was a Marine Corps boxing champion,
and we became good friends.
During his training,
I ran with him
sometimes 10 miles.

Then Martin Luther King, Jr. was killed.
I came back to the base in mid-afternoon
on April 4, 1968,
and Boonie was crying.
Here was a hardcore combat Marine,
6', 6", weighing 200 pounds
and tough as nails,
crying like a baby.
He told me, "They've killed our king."
I didn't catch on at first. "What king?"
"Martin Luther King, Jr."

My whole body sank.
I knew we were in deep trouble
in a barracks where everybody was armed.
We kept M-1 rifles and 45 caliber pistols
in our lockers.

I could hear rifles being locked and loaded
out in the squad bay.
Black guys were loading up.
"We can't let this happen!"
I pleaded to Boonie.
"Those guys are my brothers.
We fought together
and lived through a war."

We had to go out there and take control.
The whole place was in chaos,
and the commanders were gone.
It was up to us
to keep an all-out war from happening
in our barracks.

Everybody was mustering up
getting ready to raise hell,
but we talked our guys down.

We mobilized into a riot patrol squad,
and when our command came back
we headed out
into the streets of San Francisco
to try to quell the violence.

That was awful.
We had holstered 45 caliber pistols
we couldn't use,
and billy clubs.
We didn't have helmets
or flak jackets.
We wore cloth utility hats,
and were getting stoned
with bricks and rocks.

After fighting in a civil war in Vietnam,
that I found out
many of our populace was against,
now we were in combat
against our own people
in our own country.

I couldn't take it anymore,
but still had six months left
of my tour of duty
before I could go home.

Busted

Two or three days after
Martin Luther King, Jr. was killed
me and another guy went out to a bar
and got hammered big time.

I had a motorcycle
and had been up for hours.
I came back that morning
to this top-secret base
doing 90 miles an hour.

I flew through the gate,
laid the bike down sideways
and slid to a stop,
putting on a show for the guys on duty.
We all knew each other.

There happened to be a lieutenant
standing there checking posts,
and I got in trouble.
He turned me in.

Next morning I had to meet
with a full bird colonel,
that's one step down from a general.

Standing in front of him during office hours
was like going to court.
The Colonel read off my two violations.
One for running the gate,
and one for not showing up for patrol.

I was supposed to take a crew
out on the streets
that morning.

He asked me,
"Do you have anything to say for yourself?"
I answered,
"No Sir, I'm not denying what you read
out to me,
but I made it plain
I didn't want this type of duty anymore.
I fought in a civil war in a foreign country.

I'll be god-damned
if I'm going to come back to America
and fight a civil war on the streets
of my own country.
People are getting their heads bashed in.
It's going to turn into a shooting war,
and I don't want any part of it."
He said, "That's your orders."

Places were burning down.
That's the way it was
after Martin Luther King, Jr. was killed
in April 1968.
It was a scary time.

Blacks were still being sprayed down
with firehoses in Mississippi.
It was rough,
and I didn't figure I was going to live
to be 25 or 30 years old.

I went AWOL
and got drunk again,
chugged who knows how many whiskeys,
and was passed out in bed
when my crew mustered up.
The gunnery sergeant rolled me out
and took me down to the Colonel.

They took a stripe from me.
It was humiliating.
I'd worked hard for my rank
and was proud of it.

I just wasn't going back
out on the streets again.

R and R

Getting busted was a good thing for me.
I got reassigned
to a different duty station,
part of the same barracks, but 20 miles away.

It was another top secret base on an island
surrounded by marshland and water,
and also run by the Navy.
I was an MP at the gate.

I had my own room
with a nice bed.
I'd eat in a kitchen that was like a restaurant.
You didn't go through a line
and have slop put on your plate.

You got good food.
In the morning the cooks made eggs
the way you wanted,
with four or five choices of meat.

There was a regulation-sized pool,
and it was a hot time of year.
It was almost like R and R.

An office guy told me
the reason for all this
was the Marines wanted me to reenlist.
They were trying to butter me up.

If I signed up
I would get a $13,000 bonus,
which was a lot of money back then,
plus a promotion.

They'd send me back to Vietnam
to be a sniper in a reconnaissance unit.

Life expectancy wasn't very good.
If you were out in the field
you might last a week.
I wasn't going for it.

I had my motorcycle and a car,
and the city of Napa was close.
I had some good friends in Napa.
That island is where
I served out my tour.

Epilogue

Theresa: Party House

I was living with three girls on 8th Street.
Larry was living with four guys
at 601 W Front Street,
across from a small store
called Little Bo Beers.

He'd moved to Traverse City
about a month before.
With five guys living together,
it was a party house.

I was a Cher look-alike
wearing bell-bottoms.
I had a job with Michigan Bell
as a long-distance
telephone operator.
Other than dancing at Tanz Haus,
I was a good girl.

I wasn't politically involved
about the Vietnam War at all.
My brother-in-law, Wayne,
served before Larry.
So I knew there was a war
and I saw the news on TV.

My friend, Sherri
had gone over to their house
and met Larry,
or gone out with him.

She said to me,
"Theresa, I met this Italian guy.
I think you two would really hit it off
and like each other."

So, I went over to 601 W Front Street.
There was another Italian guy there
and I got them mixed up.
When I finally met Larry
I saw a lot of drinking and wildness.

That was my introduction
to my future husband.
He'd flirt with me a little bit,
but I couldn't stand him.

About a week later
a bunch of us were at this house.
I was sitting on the couch
and he was sitting on the floor.
He used to smoke
and had one of those Zippo lighters.
He was flipping it open
to light a cigarette
while telling a story.

By then I was dating one of the guys
he lived with.
I sat there and looked at him
from that angle.
He'd been ignoring me for days
because I wouldn't react to him.

I watched him light that cigarette
and thought, "You know,
he's pretty good looking."
I watched him smoke his cigarette
and tell his story.

Later that night we got together
and switched dates.
He asked someone else
to take the other girl home.

We kissed,
and the next night was our first date.

Theresa: In Love

I was in love with Larry before I knew
he'd been in Vietnam.
I didn't really know what that meant.
We didn't watch the news.

I'd be with him after work
till the wee hours of the morning.
We didn't live together,

but couldn't be apart.
We were together
every single night.

We'd go to the J & S restaurant
at two in the morning
for cheeseburgers and fries.
I'd go home to my apartment on 8th Street
at three or four a.m.,
then go to work
after three hours of sleep.

My parents approved,
Mom voiced a slight ripple of concern
when she commented
about him being in the war,
but Dad loved Larry,
and I was close to my father.

Dad knew him to be a good man
right from the get go.
He homed in on that.

They went duck hunting
and rabbit hunting together.

Theresa: Early Marriage

I graduated in 1968
and met Larry a year later.
We were married within four months
in the summer of 1969.
I was 19 and he was 22.

Looking back,
I'd have to say I married a stranger.
I knew nothing about his life.
All I knew is that I loved him
with all my heart.

He's the only young man I instinctively trusted.
I didn't see any warning signs
until after we were married.

I always knew he was a good man,
a good husband with a good heart.

I was a young wife and mother
when all these scary symptoms with Larry
started going on.
I can remember the exact time
this man said, "F--- you!"
It was like, "What!
My husband wouldn't say that to me!"
I didn't understand
what happened in the war
or what Post Traumatic Stress Disorder was.

There was no explanation
for my husband's behavior,
the danger and violence
going on in our lives.
It was like being in a lifeboat without oars.

He didn't tame down for 20 years.
He was always on the edge,
on that line,
until he toned down his drinking.

Theresa: The List

Shell Shock, Soldier's Heart, Battle Fatigue,
Post-Traumatic Stress
wasn't talked about.
There wasn't a name for the silence.

In the mid 1970's
we received a questionnaire
from the state government
with a list of questions dealing with PTSD.

"Do you have any of these symptoms?"
There were 32 boxes
you could check.

We stood side by side
and read the list.
My husband looked at me
and honestly said, "I could check
every one of these boxes."

I agreed.
Larry had all the symptoms
of Post-Traumatic Stress.

Post-Traumatic Stress Disorder

You learn how to hide things,
not knowingly.

After I was married I figured,
"Now I've got a chance."
Before I met Theresa
I didn't expect to live past 25 or 30.

She absolutely saved me.
No question about it.

All the young Traverse City people
were eager to get out.
There wasn't a lot of opportunity here.
I thought, "I'm in this peaceful town.
Man, I'm here to stay."

But I started having trouble
with anger,
hyper-vigilance,
not trusting being around other people,
battle flashbacks and nightmares.
I would punch walls out
and do things I'm not proud of.

Up until 1980, I wouldn't associate
with another Vietnam veteran.
I couldn't be around them.
I didn't want anything that would remind me
of my war past.

I hit the bottle.
It was the only relief I could get.
I wasn't much
on taking prescription medicine,
but I'd have a few drinks
and the pain would go away.

I'd wake up in the night after drinking,
and I'd feel worse.
It was like Catch 22. So I quit everything.

What Was This?

I was highly exposed to Agent Orange
in Vietnam,
and both our sons were born
with birth defects,
one serious.
After surgeries, they both recovered
and live normal lives.

There was an Agent Orange conference
in Gaylord.
Theresa said we should go
to find out about this.

A lot of Vietnam vets were there,
30 or more of them.
I felt real uncomfortable,
but toughed it out.

I got to talking with a couple guys
from Traverse City
and felt better.

Vietnam Veterans of America
was starting up.
We formed our own group in Traverse City,
kind of like the VFW,
but our own organization.
I started going to meetings
and paying dues.

More and more guys started coming.
We'd be talking about problems
we were having
with anger, hyper-vigilance,
not trusting being with groups of people,
flashbacks and nightmares.
All these symptoms
a lot of us carried.

What the hell was this?
Why were we all so similar?

Terrible Stories

In certain parts of Vietnam
there were leeches all over.
I told the story one night at Stone Circle
about leeches
crawling up our asses,
and having to burn them out of each other
with lit cigarettes.
The host got upset.

That's one thing about a veteran
who's lived through the hellish things
some of us have.
The experiences are meaningless to us,
and we don't understand
the stories might offend other people.
I finally realized that.

At first you don't talk about your memories.
You don't talk to anybody.
Then you want to talk
and get it all out
because it's healing.
You get carried away
and think the words are no big deal.

Some of the stories that are funny to veterans
are terrible to other people.

I'll Never Go Back

I'm not going back there.
You'd get caught up in the voodoo
of that place.

A friend of mine went back
summer before last.
There were twelve of them,
all Army guys
wanting to visit old battlefields.

They climbed up
a tall rocky kind of mountain,
like you'd have in Arizona,
not the Rockies,
and were standing on top.

They started looking around.
There were twelve guys,
but they could only find eleven.
So they started searching
for their buddy.
Turns out he had fallen off
and was killed.
It messed up their whole trip.

Now

I'm at a point in my life
where I don't think like I used to.
I've been out of that mindset
for a long time.

I have a lot of friends
who resisted the war,
and have a great deal
of respect for them.

The Ceremony

I went to the Vietnam Memorial
when I was in Washington D.C.
for the film, *Welcome Home*, in 2017.
I've been there four or five times,
and looked up most of the guys.

On Memorial Day weekend
it was crowded,
and I needed help.
They have guides wearing vests
so you know who they are.

I walked up to this guide
and asked him
if he'd look up a name.
It was a different Martinez
who was killed next to me
during the Battle of Hastings;
Pedro Martinez was his name.
I wanted to look up Pedro.

I already knew
where my other Martinez buddy was.
His name was Toto Jesus Martinez.

A couple guides were helping me
and asked,
"Have you been here before?"
"Yes," I answered, "and this time
I want to find Pedro."
While they were looking him up,
this lady and guy
came up to me
and asked about my service.

I told them
I was a Marine in Vietnam,
and had 20 some friends on this wall.

They held a little ceremony
and honored me with a pin.

I couldn't believe it.
"What the hell is going on here?"
My wife was with me,
and my sister, and her husband.
That was kind of cool.

Healing

Seeking out and destroying an enemy is a grueling business. Being in a combat zone is hard work under miserable, dangerous conditions. It's challenging to do long range patrols on foot, humping heavy gear while being vigilant of the enemy at all times and dealing with rough terrain like a desert, jungle, or mountain. You work long hours in an environment that wants to kill you, let alone the enemy. You deal with extreme temperatures, deadly insects, snakes, animals, toxic fumes, chemicals, contaminated water and food. Lack of enough supplies, marginal shelter and sleep deprivation is common.

Security, freedom and comfort doesn't exist in close combat situations. You are under rule of command 24/7. You shut up, do what you are told, and try to stay alive to help the troops that are close to you to survive.

The enemy is resourceful. They speak the native language, know the lay of the land, are well trained, disciplined and equipped. Their only rule of engagement is to kill or hurt an American in any way that they can. The enemy has very little value of life whether it is themselves or their own people. The only thing that matters to them is to kill people that get in their way or don't think the same way as they do.

If you are to survive in combat, you can't get hung up on emotion. This can cause you to lose your edge. You must react to situations instantly, instinctively, with no time to grieve over casualties. Split seconds can mean life or death. Every battle is different but every battle is chaos. Survival depends on skill, instinct, and divine intervention. Grief comes later when the smoke clears.

The term Post Traumatic Stress Disorder (PTSD) came into use in the 1970's due to the diagnosis of veterans of the Vietnam War.

It's not the veterans that are disordered, but the war that was chaotic and disordered. Many of the people that fought in the war came back injured mentally and physically. The term PTSD is insulting, in my opinion. It's written in all of the books and manuals so we are stuck with it. I, with the other veterans went off and did our patriotic duty. We brought home our 58,148 killed in action and 304,000 wounded and went on with our lives. We asked for nothing but to be welcomed home and not be characterized as disordered or looked down on because the outcome of the war didn't support the political goals of our leaders.

A person's experience in combat is an advancement into a higher state of being. You learn things about yourself that you would never have known: your strengths, your weaknesses, how you react in extreme danger. You learn how to understand and appreciate small things and live life feeling grateful to be alive, safe, and free.

Mental health professionals talk about Post Traumatic Stress Disorder, Traumatic Brain Injury (TBI) and Moral Injury as separate conditions, which they are. But to the person that is living with a diagnosis of all three, it can be hard to separate them. The awareness of TBI and PTSD is not new. A large percentage of veterans that have a brain injury also have PTSD. But what about Moral Injury being added to the mix?

Moral Injury is not discussed a lot yet. This is something that is very serious and needs to be addressed by health care professionals in a more aggressive manner. This injury hits you at the very core of your being. It does damage to your soul, your spirit, your beliefs, and your mental being. More common than not, combat veterans have experienced things that are too grim to talk about. These memories stay bottled up inside, never to be revealed to anyone.

The symptoms of these three injuries overlap. What term is used when a person is diagnosed with all three? Is it treated differently? I can't answer these questions. I am not an authority on brain injury. Nor am I a doctor of any sort. The subject is so complicated, it may not be good for me that I express my views any further. If you look up any of the terms PTSD, TBI, or Moral Injury on the internet, a mountain of information will come up.

I am a veterans' advocate, peer counselor, and guide. I do my best to pass on information, answer questions, and help when possible. Sometimes a person will pick up on one sentence that is said and it can turn a life around for the better.

I am asked to speak to groups of people about veteran issues. Over the years I have put together 10 talking points that I call the Foundation for Healing. The 10 short paragraphs have been well received and bring up good conversation leading to questions and answers.

Foundation for Healing (10 steps)

1   Sleep
Sleep is often overlooked in today's culture. The average American gets between 6 and 7 hours of sleep. The human body needs 8 or 9 hours to repair and replace cells. Research shows that good restorative Rapid Eye Movement sleep is very important in a person's mental health and well being.

2   Daily Exercise
Exercise helps you to survive emotionally and physically. Exercise helps the body to release good endorphins that reduce stress. It strengthens our cardiovascular system, helps keep our weight down, sculpts our body making us look better, and builds our self-confidence. Any exercise done outside such as walking or hiking in nature among the trees, plants, birds, and animals helps reduce anxiety and brings peace of mind.

3   Proper Nutrition and Hydration
We are living organisms that require proper nutrition and water. What we put into our bodies determines the status of our health. When we are under stress, physical or emotional,

it is even more important to eat nutritional food. Work with a nutritionist to evaluate your habits and provide strategies for change, if needed. It's best to try to limit processed, junk and fast food. Hydration is a key for avoiding mood swings, cravings, overeating, headaches, body aches and just feeling out-of-sorts. Every organ and cell in your body needs water. Most health authorities recommend eight 8-ounce glasses per day, which is easily accomplished with drinking the equivalent of two, quart-size containers daily.

4. **Substance Abuse**
   Using alcohol and drugs to self-medicate is extremely dangerous. Many military veterans use alcohol or drugs. Some use both to cope with and dull symptoms of PTSD, but in fact, they create further problems with memory. Their use alters judgement, slows reactions, affects cognition and behavior. The only safe amount of alcohol is none. Drugs should only be prescribed by a mental health professional. Drugs must be monitored very closely between you and your provider. A lot of guess work is involved to start out. What works for some people may not be good for you. If you become impaired in any way, it is your responsibility to communicate with your doctor. You are working as a team and you are in charge.

5. **Build a Support Network**
   All human challenges are easier with caring people by your side. Encircle yourself with family and friends that you can trust with your thoughts and feelings. Don't waste time on people that don't have your best interest in mind, or people that want to disagree and argue with you a lot.

6. **Find an accredited Veterans Service Officer (VSO)**
   The VA system can be difficult to understand and access. A Veterans Service Officer can be of great service to you with information and direction on helping you to apply for the many benefits that you have earned and deserve. Your VSO types the

many VA forms required by the VA and helps you acquire your military records needed for documentation. This is a free service that is provided by local government and military organizations such as the VFW, American Legion or Disabled American Veterans (DAV). Search out a recommended VSO and make an appointment.

7 **Join a Military Organization**
Veterans have a tendency to isolate themselves and avoid association with groups of people. In today's society, it's important to network with other people. Being involved in a veteran's organization can be a valuable asset that provides information, peer support, and camaraderie. The American Legion, Veterans of Foreign Wars (VFW), Disabled American Veterans (DAV), Vietnam Veterans of America (VVA), Military Order of the Purple Heart (MOPH), American Military League (AML), and Student Veterans of America are good organizations. Being involved with a veterans' non-profit organization can also be beneficial.

8 **Group Therapy**
Attending group therapy is, in my mind, one of the most positive things that a veteran can do to begin healing from PTSD. Being in a group of 2-to-12 vets who have gone through experiences similar to yours can be very beneficial. Being with others who share their experiences and hearing how they have coped with issues similar to yours is very interesting and informative. After a few meetings, the group begins to feel like a band of brothers. You become friends outside of the meetings, socializing and doing things to help each other. The VA is dedicated to providing and supporting individual and peer group meetings that I highly recommend.

9 **Equine Therapy**
Equine therapy is a group therapy that is held at a horse ranch, allowing for interactions between veterans and horses. In col-

laboration with the VA, counseling is provided to veterans. I personally went through the course and was trained as a mentor. I initially signed up through the VA for a ten-week program because of my love of animals and nature. At first it was a bit strange, being around and learning about big horses. There were eight veterans and half of them were nervous because they had never been around horses. After a couple of classes, everyone became at ease. We all began to enjoy and look forward to time in the open-air environment, the camaraderie, the benefits of group therapy, the learning about big animals, and new friendships being created. All make for a true healing experience.

10 Write to Heal

The VA offers a treatment for PTSD called Prolonged Exposure Therapy (PET). The treatment consists of sitting with a therapist that is recording your war experiences. You talk about memories that bother you the most. After a one-hour session is over, the therapist gives you a copy of the recording. Everyday for a week, you play this recording over several times a day. In one week you return to the VA office and record another tape and do the same thing. The next week the same. The treatment lasts for 10-12 weeks. After listening to these graphic recordings, your anxiety fades. It's like watching a scary movie over and over. After a while, it's not scary anymore.

Writing is much like PET. In 2013, the VA scientists published research on what they call Written Exposure Therapy. Therapeutic writing is an art. It's very personal to write about your deepest thoughts and feelings. The writing that comes from your soul is very healing. I write with pen and paper. This way I am totally connected with no distractions of a machine banging away and sometimes doing what it wants causing me to be distracted. When you write down your honest memories and feelings, then put it aside for a day or two before re-reading it, you always learn something new about yourself. It may be good or it may be bad. The good amazes you. The bad you change.

The Man in the Arena
By Theodore Roosevelt

It is not the critic who counts, not the man who points out how the strong man stumbles, or where the doer of deeds could have done them better.

The credit belongs to the man who is actually in the arena, whose face is marred by dust and sweat and blood; who strives valiantly; who errs, who comes short again and again, because there is no effort without error and shortcoming; but who does actually strive to do the deeds; who knows great enthusiasm, the great devotions; who spends himself in a worthy cause;

who at the best knows in the end the triumph of high achievement, and who at the worst, if he fails, at least fails while daring greatly, so that his place shall never be with those cold and timid souls who neither know victory nor defeat.

From a speech entitled *Citizenship In a Republic*, by Theodore Roosevelt, delivered at the Sorbonne in Paris, France, on April 23, 1910.

If this book has been helpful to you,
we recommend you point your browser to:

For the US Department of Veterans affairs:

https://www.va.gov

For Vietnam Veterans of America:

https://vva.org

For Veterans of Foreign Wars:

https://www.vfw.org/

For The American Legion:

https://www.legion.org/education

This book was published by:

https://www.parkhurstbrothers.com

To Order TRUE HARD:
Lelito Publications
P.O. Box #52
Williamsburg, MI. 49690
lelitopublications@gmail.com
www.lelitopublications.com